LET YOUR Daddy Lift YOU UP

Healing "Daddy Issues" to Build Healthy Relationships

ARLENE L. CONNELLY
FOREWORD BY: HENRY FERNANDEZ

Healing "Daddy Issues"
To Build Healthy Relationships

ARLENE L. CONNELLY

© 2018 Divine Works Publishing

Let Your Daddy Lift You Up

ALL RIGHTS RESERVED. No part of this publication may be reproduced, stored in a retrieval system, or transmitted in any form or by any means, electronic mechanical, photocopying, recording or otherwise without the prior permission of the publisher or in accordance with the provisions of the Copyright, Designs and Patents Act 1988 or under the terms of any license permitting limited copying issued by the Copyright Licensing Agency.

The views expressed in this work are solely those of the author and do not necessarily reflect the views of the publisher, the publisher hereby disclaims any responsibility for them.

ISBN-13: 978-1-949105-09-4 (paperback)

Holy Bible, New International Version®, NIV; King James Version®, KJV Copyright ©1973 1978, 1984, 2011 by Biblica, Inc.® Used by permission. All Rights Reserved Worldwide.

Published by:
Divine Works Publishing
Royal Palm Beach, Florida USA

www.DivineWorksPublishing.com
561-990-2665

Dedication

This book is dedicated to my daughter, Zakiya Becca—you are my inspiration and my greatest motivation. You are the best, and I thank God for entrusting me to parent one of His special gifts to the world. It is an honor and a privilege to be your mom. Rise up and let your light shine, your voice heard and your presence transform those who come in contact with you. To Lance Becca, for supporting, encouraging, and journeying with me for over 35 years even as life took us in different directions. Your friendship remained constant. I appreciate you for the example you have provided of a loving and devoted father.

To all the youth and families I have encountered over my 27+ years of developing, implementing and monitoring community based programs. I witnessed the residual impact of brokenness in the absence of the safety and support of a loving father and/or stable home. I saw the reflection of my life through you and connect to your pain. I have also learned so much from you about myself. Thank you. You remind me daily that the first and most important relationship is the one developed between parent and child. You have expressed that this is one of your greatest challenges and I see the impact. I write this for you.

To all those who have weathered the storms of life and have been beaten, broken, tattered, torn, uprooted, displaced and searching for the covering found in the arms of a loving father —I salute you. You have travailed.

To my mom, I seek daily to honor you in all that I do. In your HONOR!

I dedicate this book back to My DADDY- God, The Creator, The Source, The Divine... thank You for guiding me through this pathway and using me as Your vessel.

Acknowledgments

To the support systems that God placed in my life— individuals who stepped in and embraced me as part of their family, loved and supported me—Dorothy Becca, Dianne Becca, Lance Becca & the entire Becca Family. The love and support you have extended to me since childhood into adulthood has helped to sustain me when I felt like giving up.

Thank you, Mr. West and Darren Morton for your steadfast love and support. Angela Stoute–God's Angel–sent to answer the prayers of a broken woman. Thank you for opening the doors to your home and heart and welcoming me home to rest. Lorraine Campbell and Athelene Collins-AC[2], my sister from another mother, thank you for your love, and friendship. Donna Marshall, my prayer accountability partner. Our prayers have availed much! Winsome Mundy, thank you for believing in me and investing in the realization of this book. To my dear sisters, Debbie, Susan, and Michele, we have travailed, persevered, and exemplify the power of resiliency. Thank you to my Cousin Dawn, for searching us out and opening the portal for reconciliation. To Michael J. Drummond for your friendship, love, and support. I appreciate you and thank God for your presence in my life!

Dr. Belinda John, thank you for continually training, guiding, inspiring, and motivating me. My heart overflows with gratitude for your presence in my life.

Thanking God for the divine connection and answered prayers found in the sisterhood of women in Daughters of Zion–Women of Destiny.

A special thanks to Lelia Fore for capturing the vision for my book cover.

The inspirational teachers I have encountered on my journey with a special acknowledgment to Bishop T.D. Jakes, Dean Frank W. Smith, and the late Dr. Myles Munroe, thank you for exposing me to the knowledge of self, history, and the wisdom of God's Word.

My spiritual father–Bishop Henry Fernandez. Thank you for connecting me to Jesus. You have imparted the wisdom of a father.

Endorsements

Let Your Daddy Lift You Up, is a riveting articulation of one woman's journey to a healthy self despite the feelings of abandonment, loneliness and loss of self through broken relationship and blindness to a new awakening. The search for our earthly father's love can have devastating effects on our journey to a healthy us. But, we have the power to overcome these adversities in life through a greater understanding of our challenges and how healing is transformative. This book will help the reader gain new insight of God's desires for each human being to have a strong relationship with self and Him, as an omnipresent, omniscient, and omnipotent God. Our "Daddy issues" with our earthly fathers never forsake access to God's promise to always be there, know our needs, and lift us up. The words in this book offer practical and simplistic approaches to overcome our relationship and reconciliation issues (abandonment, and sense of rejection) and seek new revelations about God's never-changing and infallible promise to make us whole.

Rev. Dr. Darren M. Morton, Ed.D
Pastor, Macedonia Baptist Church, Mt. Vernon, NY
Assistant Adjunct Professor, College of New Rochelle, NY

Coming from a faith-filled home where both parents worshipped daily, my childhood was calm, peaceful, and well structured. Yet, after reading just a chapter, I realized this insight would be beneficial for all. The forgiveness for others begins with the forgiveness for self, and Arlene addresses this in a unique fashion. Spirit has spoken through Arlene, may her words bring you healing.

Reverend Dr. Louise Morley
Ombudsman, Keiser University

Let Your Daddy Lift You Up, is a biographical sketch of a small word, 'let'; wrestling through the truth of an expectation that is squarely placed upon the author. There is the author; and then; there is the Author! The wrestle and struggle is for the author to surrender to the expectations of the Author. This book is a literary personalization for vulnerability to obey. The Author never overrides the author. It's a choice. Success belongs to the book; the battle is over, the author is transparent, 'let' submits the consequences of the absentee daddy. There is now less of life's traffic for pain and disappointment and even failures. Who celebrates failure? Truth is to be measured by the omnipresence of the Author, He never leaves. He's always going where's He's coming from to get to; where He is, to find out, He's already there! The truth of survival, recovery and reclamation is written in this book. The fight isn't over. It's your turn. Read! The bell still didn't ring!

Nevilon J. Meadows, CEO
Men Under Development (M.U.D.), Inc.

Table of Contents

Foreword *xiii*

Preface *xv*

Introduction *xvii*

1| The Daddy Void: An Inside Look   1

2| Who's Your Daddy?   13

3| Learning to Love Me   29

4| The Path Towards Healing   37

5| Getting From Here to There   47

6| Can I Trust You?   57

7| Calling Out to Him   61

8| Resting on His Shoulders   69

About The Author   79

Foreword

Arlene Connelly knows what it's like to be angry. As an 11-year-old child, she was angry that God didn't answer her prayer and save her sick mother from dying. In her later years, angry that growing up she had no father figure in her life to lift her up—to help guide her through some of her most difficult years and help her to grow and mature into a godly woman.

"I was angry because I could not understand where He was, why did He not protect me," Arlene writes in this amazingly revealing book. "All I knew was the piercing pain of a child who longed for love and protection from those who were entrusted to take care of me and provide a safe place for me to grow... If I had a father or a strong male in my life, who truly loved and protected me, looked out for me, many of the situations that I experienced as a child growing-up and into adulthood, would have been different."

In this insightful portrayal of her life, Arlene reflects on the "Daddy Issues" she endured that kept her living in obscurity. With clear revelation that could have only come from God, through His precious Holy Spirit, she unpacks truths that are sure to provide refreshing, renewal and restoration to anyone dealing with issues resulting from the absence of a father figure in their life.

In *Let Your Daddy Lift You Up*, Arlene shares how she came to understand that, despite how dim things may seem, no matter how alone you may feel, God, our Heavenly Father, has never left us. He's always there and always ready to take on the cares of life so we don't have to. "As I looked back and reflected on all that I had been through; that feeling of loneliness, longing, the void and emptiness, the anger and resentment I have felt for not having the safety of a loving father, He (my Heavenly Daddy) was there."

This book speaks to the hearts of many who, like Arlene, have suffered the pain of rejection and loneliness. Read it, and let the revelation God has given her saturate your spirit so that you can experience His peace and freedom.

—Bishop Henry B. Fernandez
Senior Pastor, The Faith Center Ministries–Sunrise, Florida

Preface

It was early one beautiful morning. I retreated to my favorite place, a space in which I find great peace and joy, where I find rest and bask in the magnificence of God's glory; my sacred retreat and place of solace—the beach. I rolled out my mat, laid on my back, stretched my hands towards the beautiful blue sky and immediately the idea for this book dropped into my spirit. I heard these words resonate from deep within, "let your daddy lift you up".

The vision that came to me was that of a child crying, reaching, stretching with a deep yearning, calling out to their father "daddy, daddy, lift me up daddy... daddy.... daddy... lift me up". With an earnest intensity in their request and a jovial smile upon their face. Their hands outstretched and reaching for their father, insisting, "daddy, daddy lift me up. Up daddy, UP! I want to go UP". As their daddy reaches down and picks them up, their eyes are full of excitement and joy; they are filled with glee as they are lifted to rest upon their daddy's shoulders. Their eyes open wide as they delight in a new view, from this elevated position, and are able to see further than their eyes could have seen before. I never experienced this personally, as my earthly father was not around to lift me up. However, a prevailing thought for me at that moment, became how my Heavenly Father had always been there and continuously lifted me up throughout my life.

I then heard in my spirit the chapters for this book. First, in order to cry out and ask your daddy to lift you up, you must know your daddy. Who is your daddy, do you know him? Second, a request must be made, requiring communication, asking for what you want; followed by an acknowledgment from your daddy that he heard you. Third, a relationship assures trust has been established, and you have to know that your daddy can carry you. Fourth, with expanded vision, you are elevated to a higher level where you can see past the obstacles, that were impeding your vision, and obstructing your view.

Fifth, is embracing and fully experiencing the joy and contentment of being elevated and basking in the opportunity to rest upon his shoulders.

What I did not consider at the moment and would require time to process was: why am I being told to "LET" my daddy lift me up", what is being said here? As I gave it more thought, I wondered why God was saying this to me? Let Your Daddy Lift You UP? Hasn't He already lifted me up? A series of questions flooded my mind...

> What am I still holding on to, and what have I not yet released?
> Where am I still burdened, heavy, or weighted?
> What have I picked up or never let go of?
> Is there a higher place You are taking me Lord?
> Is it time for my life to go higher in You?
> Is there a deeper level that God desires to take me?
> If so, how will I get there? What do I need to do?

The initial excitement I was feeling about this book assignment was beginning to dissipate. In addition to discussing this topic of being lifted up by daddy, this book necessitates me to share my experiences with both my heavenly and earthly fathers.

Introduction

I can vividly remember a few months after moving to South Florida from New York being invited to a church named Plantation Worship Center, now The Faith Center. After several invitations, one Sunday morning in 1998, this skeptic, non-trusting, and uninterested woman, stepped into the doors of this church. Upon arrival, I was greeted warmly and embraced like I was seeing family whom I had not seen in a long time. At that time in my life, I was heart-broken, angry, disappointed and feeling lost. My life seemed uncertain after wedding plans were canceled and a long, intensive relationship, to a wonderful man came to an end. Church was not a place I was connected to and God was not one of my favorite people. I was an angry person, angry at God for not answering the prayers of an 11 year old child to - save my mother, and take away the pain and suffering she was experiencing. God allowed her to die. I was angry because I could not understand where He was and why He had not protected me. All I knew was the piercing pain of a child who longed for love and protection from those who were entrusted to take care of me and provide a safe place for me to grow. This was the space I was in when I encountered Bishop Henry Fernandez. There was something different about him. He spoke with zeal and a refreshing honesty that I had not heard before; a teacher who shared the Word of God with applicable, simplistic clarity. He encouraged the congregation to develop a relationship with God, to know His Word for ourselves. I had not heard that before, it was my understanding that I could only connect with God through a priest. It was probably my fourth visit and on this day Bishop Fernandez said to the congregation, "take a look back over your life and see how your Father [God] has been there. He took it a step further and asked everyone to stand, turn our heads back and take a flashback over our lives to see, identify, and acknowledge the presence of our Father with us. The hand, presence, covering, and love of God had been in our lives. It was in that moment that I looked back and was able to see, for the first time, a different vision of my life. I pictured all the stages of my life; through trials and turbulence, pain and distress, hurt and disappointment... the real joys and sorrows, that even when I didn't know Him, He was there. As I looked back and reflected on all that I had been through; that feeling of loneliness, longing, the void and emptiness, the anger and resentment I had felt for not having the safety of a loving father, He (my Heavenly Daddy) was there.

In that moment, I was able to acknowledge and know that I was still standing. I am still here. I had the opportunity to look back and see how far I had come. I wept, I don't even know for how long, that I called out and cried out to God... THANK YOU! THANK YOU! For even when I didn't know You, You were there. You loved me when I didn't know how to give You the praise, honor, acknowledgement, and recognition You are due... You've been there all the time; that was a turning point for me. I was now able to look back at my life through new lenses. I could see, touch and feel the weight and pain of the journey; but the intense bitterness of my pain has been replaced with the sweet taste of joy, knowing that my Heavenly Father saw me through it all. I am stronger for the journey, stronger for the experiences, that the good and the bad, tragic and piercing pain, grief/sorrows, intense anger and resentment, every hurt, every disappointment, every negative experience; I am the sum total of all those experiences- Gestalt. They have helped craft and shape me. I am, because of my journey. It didn't break me, I did not shatter in to a thousand pieces. Broken, bruised, chipped, cracked, sometimes peeling, from experiencing the intense heat of the fire... I began a journey of learning more about His love for me. How He saw me, His masterpiece; I, Arlene crafted in the hands of the master potter; stand before you, here in this moment, with all my imperfections. I have weathered the storms, and have an enduring resilient spirit, I'm stronger today. I can testify to His goodness, His grace, His mercy, and His love everlasting.

I have often said to others that I believed, if I had a father or a strong male in my life, who truly loved and protected me, and looked out for me during many of the situations that I experienced as a child, growing-up, and into adulthood, I would have been different. There is something to be said for how someone treats you, when they know you are loved and protected. They will think twice about how they treat you if they know someone is looking out for you and will hold them accountable for treating you as the special gift that you are.

So here I am, I cry out to You Father, my hands lifted up in full surrender and thanksgiving, reaching out to You, giving praise to You daddy, daddy, I thank You for lifting me. For I have been stronger as I sat on Your shoulders. I know that You are calling me, I know Your voice, You know my voice and I know how to converse with You. I know what it feels like to be in Your presence. I am confident knowing that You are there. I am confident knowing from experience that You can carry me, even with my heavy-weighted burdens.

I used to wonder as I observed people who declared/professed/proclaimed their love for Christ; what that relationship was like, what have they experienced or shared that made people cry out; tears rolling down their faces, weeping, down on their knees, hands lifted up in full surrender crying out to God. I get it, I can relate. I know for myself, that spirit of gratitude, of complete and utter reverence, deep, and abiding love... Fully committed, safe surrender in His arms and on His shoulders, knowing that You God, You are with me. With us always.

As I think about this concept the song that came into my spirit, "You Raise Me Up" by Josh Groban. Read these lyrics and listen to this song.

"You Raise Me Up"

When I am down and, oh, my soul, so weary;
When troubles come and my heart burdened be;
Then I am still and wait here in the silence,
Until you come and sit awhile with me.

You raise me up, so I can stand on mountains;
You raise me up to walk on stormy seas;
I am strong when I am on your shoulders;
You raise me up to more than I can be.

I have learned what it means to be a worshipper— to fully surrender, acknowledge, and adore God at all times, and in every circumstance. I put my trust in Him and His guidance over my life. I understand and internalize that even when it's not good, it's good. God is in control. I find great joy in singing praises unto God, to worship and adore Him. As we journey together, I invite you to have a worship experience with me. I will infuse music that moves me and speaks to my soul. The words in the song "You Raise Me Up", uplifts me... Yes daddy, I am stronger when I am on Your shoulders, it is You daddy who raised me up to be more than I can be. I can see further because of You. I am elevated above my obstacles, situations and circumstances.

I wrote this book, I penned these words to those who long for healthy, loving, growth-facilitating relationships and those feeling the nudge in your spirit for healing. While facing and healing from the emotional pain of our earthly daddy, it is necessary to fully connect with our Heavenly Father. You may not know yet, but you long for Him. You were created for this.

To those who know Him and have experienced the joy and comfort of His love and seek opportunities to bask in His Glory and to those who seek and long for the love of a father, I want you to know that Your Heavenly Father is waiting for you. Your Father has never left you or forsaken you, He has been with you always. He is ever present, waiting for you to invite Him into your life for you to experience His love. For you to feel his presence you just have to call out His name, daddy, daddy, daddy! DADDY LIFT ME UP!!!

Together, let us seek clarity, revelation, and understanding; learn and experience what a relationship with our loving Father can be/is. I was dropped by those who were given the responsibility to raise me up but the Word of God says...

> *When my father and my mother forsake me, then the*
> *Lord will take me up. -Psalm 27:10*

CHAPTER 1

The Daddy Void: An Inside Look

When God gave me this book to write, I was initially filled with joy, love, and excitement. However, as I began to ponder on the title and chapters which God downloaded to me, I realized that I could not write this book and focus solely on the exhilaration which fills my heart when I think about Daddy (My Heavenly Father) lifting me up. What God was actually calling me to do was to fully surrender, unpack, release, and finally "let go" of the pain and unforgiveness which I had buried deep within my soul. This journey required me to open closed doors, hidden/secret doors that I didn't know existed and while having to answer the question, "Is there a hole in my heart, an emptiness that I am longing to fill?"

Throughout my adult life, I have spoken in front of audiences which ranged from 15-1000 or more people. I speak freely about my life's journey and how it has shaped me into the person I now am. I also acknowledge that I have done a whole lot of talking, but I question whether I have truly unpacked the emotional baggage that comes with abandonment, neglect, loss, abuse and the void of an absentee father. What might I still be holding on to that could be holding me hostage and blocking me from living a full and divinely purposeful life?

The door is now opened and as I pen these words, I am experiencing another layer of "peeling". Can I do this? Can I write about this? Why did God give this book to me?

When I pose this question to God, He answers me, a still small voice in my spirit. "I qualify you, I gave this to you. Push through and give birth to this. It is time for the author to arise for the world is in need of what I have given you to say. Step through the doors and let's see what we find". There is another level in me, this is the work that is required for you to elevate to the next level in your life. Ok Lord, let's get to work.

I can describe my family as unstable, dysfunctional, abusive and fragmented; where examples of unhealthy relationships and broken marriages exist. I am the product of being mishandled (dropped and bruised) by those who were to care for me. Void of stability, growing up with an absentee father and exposed to countless toxic experiences, I faced the difficult feelings and confronted the deep pain; and stepped into a deeper layer of self-awareness and healing. Let's unpack together and deal with the longing and thirst in our soul. Our spirits cry out in silent pain—pain that has been buried, locked away.

On this journey, let us offload and release:

1. ABANDONMENT and SENSE OF REJECTION—My emotional sensitivity and sense of self-worth is in question. I am not sure how long I was subconsciously living in the space of longing... For so long I rejected, denounced, and resented the need or desire for a father. I buried the ache deep within my heart.

2. THE WEIGHT OF PAIN AND DISAPPOINTMENT—The aching feeling deep in the fabric of your being that is left unfulfilled and lowers your expectations of life and others in an attempt to dull the pain.

3. THE LONGING TO FEEL SAFE, PROTECTED, AND COVERED—Which left unchecked can lead to a victim mindset and self-sabotaging behaviors.

4. FEELING UNLOVED—Desiring a clean, pure-intentioned, unconditional love, not tainted by lust and impure desires
   - Thirst for Validation
   - Need for Security
   - Feelings of Inadequacy
   - Unworthiness, Ugliness

The Daddy Void: An Inside Look

- Not Feeling Special or Lovable

I appreciate the opportunity to share this journey with you. Thank you for coming along. I know that I am not alone. I also know how important it is to have a solid support system as we travail through life's twists and turns, people who will remind you that you are not in this alone. I have been blessed to connect with and have developed a supportive network of people who celebrate me while I am realizing my purpose. They support, encourage, challenge and correct; they hold me accountable. As we peer into our past to gain insight— to heighten our present with an awareness of what we have gone through to get to our NOW—invite or let someone in your inner circle know that you are embarking on this journey. We are seeking to move into our future not as a victim but victorious because we travailed.

This journey of relationship with 'Daddy', is a shared experience which impacts both women and men. Most often when people speak of "Daddy Issues" they reflect on the behaviors of women. However, it is important to acknowledge that men too are impacted by the quality of relationships with their fathers or the absence of a father. They too show up with issues that impact their relationships. As we seek to build healthier more vibrant relationships in every area of our lives, this unpacking process is essential; requiring vulnerability, transparency and a willingness to feel the pain and press onward to healing and wholeness.

As I begin this reflective process I think about what we need as children. As I think about my own childhood, and the lives of the children I have encountered over the past 27 years while working with children and families, the consistency of <u>need</u> emerges.

We need to feel loved unconditionally, not because of anything we do, or how we look, not because we are 'pretty', have 'nice hair', are fair skinned, are petite not fat, but just because we are. A recognized gift, a priceless gem, special, wanted, appreciated, and accepted just as we are. A uniquely designed gift from God.

We need a sense of safety and belonging. Knowing that we have a safe place to call home, a space to retreat to, a space where unconditional love, peace, joy and care exist, where we are celebrated and supported... When this need is not met the impact is devastating on the mental and emotional development of the individual.

My personal experiences did not match or meet my needs, leaving gaping voids, holes and unfulfilled wishes. There was an aching pain that turned into numbness as the years went by and I 'learned to cope' and press forward despite this void, not fully realizing how it was showing up daily in the various areas of my life—in romantic relationships, as a parent, a friend, a sibling, an employee and in the world.

Looking In: What is the Issue? There is a Daddy Void.

As we examine our support network; the base for our grounding and development, our family; we realize the role and function of parents is essential to the foundation of each family. Each parent plays a critical role in our development. How they operate in their roles as parents, individually/as a team, and the quality of their relationship leaves a lasting impression on us. Our childhood experiences, both positive and negative, significantly impact our adulthood.

Our parents are charged with the responsibility to create a loving, safe and nurturing environment for us to learn grow and thrive in. Unfortunately for many children (like me), they have missed out on what the Center for Disease Control (CDC) refers to as "Essentials for Childhood" assuring safe, stable, nurturing relationships and environments for all children. The CDC notes that these three critical relationship qualities make a difference for children as they grow and develop:

- Safety: The extent to which a child is free from fear and secure from physical or psychological harm within their social and physical environment.
- Stability: The degree of predictability and consistency in a child's social, emotional, and physical environment.
- Nurturing: The extent to which a parent or caregiver is available and able to sensitively and consistently respond to and meet the needs of their child.

Often, people try to make us believe that we are exaggerate the impact that our childhood experiences have had on us. "We are too emotional," and "we need to just get over it." "That was then, and this is now, move on." If only it was that simple. If only the pain, brokenness, scars, and trauma could be covered up with fancy clothes, sweet perfumes, and costumes that mask the pain we feel.

Digging Deeper – Adverse Childhood Experiences

A parent's ability to fulfill their roles and responsibilities is often a challenging one and parents face various struggles daily in their ability to raise their children. If a void or imbalance is present within the family dynamic, no matter how much a parent tries to compensate for that void, the impact it creates is inevitable. The physical, mental and/or emotional presence or absence of either parent can profoundly impact the child.

As we reflect on our childhood, we will identify highs and lows. For some of us there were more lows than we care to remember. It has been comforting to learn of the work going into looking at our childhood experiences and the impact it has on who we are and how we show up in our adult lives. Our experiences are not or cannot be dismissed. They are real and our feelings are valid.

There is a body of researchers who have been focusing on digging deeper within to identify the various challenges that children are facing during their stages of development. The term used is Adverse Childhood Experiences. An Adverse Childhood Experience (ACE) describes a traumatic experience in a person's life occurring before the age of 18 that the person remembers as an adult.

The research cites that, "the effect of Adverse Childhood Experience (ACE) impacts the psychological/mental, emotional, physical and social development of an individual." I sought to explore and understand more about this research as I saw myself so clearly in it.

In a research brief issued by Child Trends in 2014, the most prevailing Adverse Childhood Experiences (ACEs) included:

—Economic hardship as the most common adverse childhood experience (ACE) reported nationally and in almost all states, followed by divorce or separation of a parent or guardian.

—Abuse of alcohol or drugs, exposure to neighborhood violence, and the occurrence of mental illness are among the most commonly-reported adverse childhood experiences in every state.

Many have buried these instances and have not paused to take a look at their own personal journey. Often, the courage to face what many may call "your personal demons", "Childhood Trauma" or "daddy issues" is challenging and traumatic. This is why the support of a trained professional maybe necessary. For some a strong support network of caring people provides the strength needed to heal. I firmly believe that this is not a journey we should take alone.

As I reviewed the checklist below I saw my childhood flash before me. I checked 7 out of the 10 questions. I put myself in the study by answering the questions used to measure ACE. If we were to reflect on our childhood and answered any of the following key questions that support the measurement of Adverse Childhood Experiences, we may find that we have endured varying levels of traumatic experiences which have influenced who and how we are today. The research brings to light the negative impact on our behavioral and physical health, and pinpoints suicide, violence or being a victim of violence, alcoholism or obesity, diabetes, heart disease and many autoimmune diseases to name a few, back to these traumas.

Measurement of Adverse Childhood Experience Questions:

Have you:

- Lived with a parent or guardian who got divorced or separated?
- Lived with a parent or guardian who died?
- Lived with a parent or guardian who served time in jail or prison?
- Lived with anyone who was mentally ill or suicidal, or severely depressed for more than a couple of weeks?
- Lived with anyone who had a problem with alcohol or drugs?

- Witnessed a parent, guardian, or other adult in the household behaving violently toward another (e.g., bullying, slapping, hitting, kicking, punching, or beating each other up)?
- Ever been the victim of violence or witnessed any violence in his or her neighborhood?
- Experienced economic hardship "somewhat often" or "very often" (i.e., the family found it hard to cover costs of food and housing)?
- Did you experience – Physical, Sexual and/or Emotional abuse
- Experienced Physical and or Emotional neglect?
- Experienced intimate partner violence?

Child Trends is a nonprofit, nonpartisan research center that studies children at all stages of development. Their mission is to improve the lives and prospects of children and youth by conducting high-quality research and sharing the resulting knowledge with practitioners and policymakers.

WOW! Isn't it eye opening when you have a personal awareness of your experiences/trauma and then see it right before you affirmed by validated research? It is noted that, "as your ACE score increases, so does your risk of health, social, and emotional problems". The research cites further, "with an ACE score of 4 or more, things start getting serious." I share this research information with you to open a doorway of awareness.

There is scientific research exploring what is happening to children during the developmental stages of their lives and how those experiences are revealing themselves in adulthood. The innocence of childhood is being ravished by trauma and toxic stress. Harvard University's Center on the Developing Child, cites the definition as such: "Toxic stress response can occur when a child experiences strong, frequent, and/or prolonged adversity—such as physical or emotional abuse, chronic neglect, caregiver substance abuse or mental illness, exposure to violence, and/or the accumulated burdens of family economic hardship—without adequate adult support". I did not have an official name or definition for what many would call a difficult childhood. However, as I dug deeper into seeking understanding and healing I found greater insights. I was seeking this heightened understanding and awareness; not to cast blame or to spend time reliving traumatic experiences that can sink me into a whirlwind of depression, but instead use this knowledge to empower myself and foster healing.

There are of course, many other types of childhood traumas such as: racism, violence (personal or observed), bullying, homelessness, surviving and recovering from a severe accident, involvement with the foster care system, involvement with the juvenile justice system, etc. All these experiences and the overall journey from infancy to adulthood leave an imprint on the adult we are today.

Below is a Sample Adverse Childhood Experiences Questionnaire, you can complete on yourself:

The most important thing to remember is that the ACE score is meant as a guideline; If you experienced other types of toxic stress over months or years, then those would likely increase your risk of health consequences.

Prior to your 18th birthday:
1. Did a parent or other adult in the household often or very often... Swear at you, insult you, put you down, or humiliate you, or act in a way that made you afraid that you might be physically hurt?
   No___   If Yes, enter 1 ___
2. Did a parent or other adult in the household often or very often... Push, grab, slap, or throw something at you? or Ever hit you so hard that you had marks or were injured? No___   If Yes, enter 1 ___
3. Did an adult or person at least 5 years older than you ever... Touch or fondle you or have you touch their body in a sexual way? or Attempt or actually have oral, anal, or vaginal intercourse with you?
   No___   If Yes, enter 1 ___
4. Did you often or very often feel that ... No one in your family loved you or thought you were important or special? or Your family didn't look out for each other, feel close to each other, or support each other? No___   If Yes, enter 1 ___
5. Did you often or very often feel that ... You didn't have enough to eat, had to wear dirty clothes, and had no one to protect you? or Your

parents were too drunk or high to take care of you or take you to the doctor if you needed it? No___ If Yes, enter 1 ___

6. Were your parents ever separated or divorced?
No___ If Yes, enter 1 ___

7. Was your mother or stepmother: Often or ever pushed, grabbed, slapped, or had something thrown at her? or ever kicked, bitten, hit with a fist, or hit with something hard? or Ever repeatedly hit over at least a few minutes or threatened with a gun or knife?
No___ If Yes, enter 1___

8. Did you live with anyone who was a problem drinker or alcoholic, or who used street drugs? No___ If Yes, enter 1 ___

9. Was a household member depressed or mentally ill, or did a household member attempt suicide? No___ If Yes, enter 1 ___

10. Did a household member go to prison? No___ If Yes, enter 1 ___

*Now add up your "Yes" answers: _____ This is your ACE Score

I embarked on a journey of reflection as I sought to unpack the baggage (that I did not fully know I was carrying) and uncover the wounds that were covered with scabs and scar tissue. I sought to no longer be numb to the pain. I was committed to confronting the trauma that instability, fragmentation and the weaknesses in my family formation, structure, and development created within me. I still am the product of an unstable foundation, which has impaired my ability to fully develop into a healthy (mentally and emotionally stable, and thriving adult). But, praise be to the Most High, for the opportunity to discover and build a relationship with Christ, for had it not been for God; I am not sure where would I be

Sources Cited:

1. **CDC Essentials for Childhood** - Reference: https://www.cdc.gov/violenceprevention/pdf/essentials_for_childhood_framework.pdf

2. **Measurement of Adverse Childhood Experience Questions:** In 2014 Child TrendsChildtrends, https://www.childtrends.org/wp-content/uploads/2014/07/Brief-adverse-childhood-experiences_FINAL.pdf

3. **Adverse Childhood Experiences Questionnaire:** *Source - https://acestoohigh.com/got-your-ace-score/

Allowing Myself to be LIFTED UP

Chapter 1: The Daddy Void

I am unpacking the Baggage - Reflect on your childhood experiences, what image, thought or incident stands out to you the most and how does it make you feel? – I felt rejected and alone when....; I remember feeling hurt and disappointed when....; I felt scared and unsafe when....; I experienced what it felt like to not feel loved when....; I breathe in the breath of life and exhale any toxic emotions associated with my childhood.

_____
_____
_____
_____
_____
_____
_____
_____
_____
_____
_____
_____
_____
_____
_____
_____
_____
_____
_____
_____
_____
_____
_____
_____
_____

MY DECLARATION:

- ✓ Today I _____, acknowledge the experiences of my childhood, and embrace my present, knowing that I survived. Each day of my life I have the opportunity to shape and design the life I want to live.

- ✓ My childhood experiences [good and bad] are tools and lessons for my journey. As I gain knowledge and understanding, I reclaim my power!

CHAPTER 2

Who's Your Daddy?

Do I Know You?
There is confidence in knowing who your daddy is.

I have been searching throughout my life for you, yet unconscious of my search, my yearning, my need, my desire, and my longing. I know that I am not alone in this search. I have encountered so many seekers throughout my walk. There is something missing, I can't fully determine what, but we know that there is a profound emptiness, which can occur, from an absentee father. When you don't know who he is and he is nameless to you; you walk around looking at the faces of men you see and wonder, could you be my daddy?

Who is my daddy? Where is my daddy? It may be a father that you only heard about, and who had not been described in a positive light. He is the sperm donor, the deadbeat, the jerk, liar, the cheat... He can also be a father who is present physically, but emotionally absent. He adds no value, but daily erodes your trust, damages your self-esteem, and makes you doubt his love. He is unreliable, inconsistent, mean-spirited and shows little to no compassion or care for you. He reminds you consistently that you are his burden, problem, and the reason his life is stuck and or the reason he has not realized his goals and dreams. You are the setback... Have pity on these types for they are missing out on the very thing— a relationship with you, which has the ability to fulfill them in ways they could never understand. Yet, they are deceived and therefore embittered.

For some, he was the good father who was ever-present, loving, kind, and caring. A father who was always there, and was a towering presence. A safe and loving arm that always cared; someone who walked with you and talked to you, and now the void caused by death, divorce or a relationship shift, leaves you empty and yearning for his presence once again.

For others, the idea of a father is but a mere observation, it is what we see or hear about. We watch TV, movies, or see our friends, the family next door and there is a father present. He seems awesome, amazing, loving, playful and fun to be around. We see how his children look at him, and his family adores him. Even when he is stern and firm, they know it comes from a place of love. They receive his correction, guidance, and teaching. He ensures that they are safe and protected. He provides structure and cares for his family. He is at every special occasion, cheering his children on. He is their biggest fan, the one who supports, encourages, motivates and inspires. If we were to create an ideal father checklist, it may include the following:

- [ ] A loving, strong, kind hearted & joyful spirit who can fix and restore broken things. We would joyfully call him, "Daddy", an endearing word used to describe a father.
- [ ] He is the individual who is the head of the household/family. [He demonstrates LEADERSHIP]
- [ ] He loves, cares and provides for his children and family [He is a PROVIDER].
- [ ] Daddy is trustworthy and reliable, caring, honest, supportive and encouraging. [He gives UNCONDITIONAL LOVE].
- [ ] Daddy is a confidence builder, who reminds us how beautiful and special we are. [He is a SELF-ESTEEM BUILDER].
- [ ] Daddy disciplines and provide structure and guidance to the family. [He lays a solid FOUNDATION].
- [ ] Daddy loves and covers his family in prayer. [He walks out his FAITH]
- [ ] Daddy's a reinforcer. Daddy is a protector. [I feel protected knowing he is there - SAFETY/SECURITY].

- [ ] Daddy challenges and pushes his children to achieve more. [HE IS MY COACH].
- [ ] To his sons and daughters, he stands as a towering example of strength, providing guidance and instruction, showing by example the characteristics/qualities and expectations of a man of wisdom, character and integrity. [MENTORSHIP]
- [ ] To his daughters he is the first man that we love and who shows us an example of what a man should be and how we should be treated by a man. [He is my EXAMPLE]
- [ ] To his son he exemplifies what it means to be a man, guides him into manhood and maleness. "Man is who I am, Manhood is what I do and Maleness is where I come from. " -N. Meadows
- [ ] Daddy in partnership with the[a] mother provides structure and balance. They function like a team – they have a vision for their family. They establish goals to realize the vision. They bring their diverse skills, talents and abilities together and work on achieving the goals set. They anchor each other, mutually supportive and grounded in love. They establish a foundational framework for the family. [PARTNERSHIP/TEAMWORK/COOPERATION]

What is noted in the above list is the ideal environment for children to grow. We acknowledge the work of individuals who parent while single. Like me, we parent while single but acknowledge that we were never a 'Single Parent'. We applaud and recognize the importance of the village or circle of people who influence and play a supportive role in the growth and development of our children.

To many of you, reading these words, you may be saying to yourself, like me... I am not able to check off many of these boxes or I never experienced that, who is this daddy you are speaking of? Do such fathers exist?

Yes, they exist. Unfortunately, though for a variety of reasons, what we often see are very few men standing in the right position and upholding this persona of a father; a daddy. The family structure for many is off balance and out of alignment.

The family structure, as God intended, is under attack and fathers have become the primary target. Healthy relationships, strong marriages, collaborative parenting and stable environments to raise children are being eroded daily as individuals struggle to build solid relationships that weather the storms of life. Simultaneously, men are struggling to find their place and understand the value and critical role they play in the family unit. Fathers are often mistakenly given a secondary role in the family and child rearing. Keep in mind that sometimes fathers aren't in the picture, not because they don't want to be, but because other factors are prohibiting them from operating in their role. There are a variety of reasons or factors that contribute to daddy absenteeism.

Reasons Fathers are Sometimes Absent:

- Evolving or Changing Definitions of Roles, Manhood, Maleness
- Weak Relationship Development
- Economics–The Challenge of Providing or Contributing to The Financial Stability of The Family
- Criminal Activity & Criminal Justice System
- Societal Infusion into The Family and Systems That Reinforce A Father's Role as a Financial Provider and Not an Active Care Giver.
- The Parental Role Is Loosely Supported by Our Societal Framework: Work Hours, School Structure, Housing Conditions, Health Care and Environment.

The following statement is cited on Fatherhood.org The National Fatherhood Initiative (NFI) is one of the nation's leading non-profit organizations working to end father absence. "There is a father absence crisis in America. According to the U.S. Census Bureau, 19.7 million children, more than 1 in 4, live without a father in the home. Consequently, there is a father factor in nearly all social ills facing America today."

The father's role is pivotal to the family and his absence places the family structure out of alignment. The family was designed by God, with each parent having a distinct role and responsibility for guiding children through the path of developing into thriving human beings. The weight of raising children has been resting heavily upon mothers. The absence or void of a help mate/partner/supportive member of the team, stresses the mother as she tries to juggle both roles. The reality is that mothers can't be fathers. We were meant to do this together, fully present and active in the process. There is a battle to preserve, fortify, and rebuild the family and reclaim its place as the central focus for our development as a society. It is a battle we cannot afford to lose.

The position of the father has been shaken and many individuals, families, people like you and me hearing this description of father, of what can or should be and are wondering "where is he? Where is my dad? Where is the daddy figure? Who can I acknowledge and call my father?" It may be a challenge to acknowledge or identify the concept of father and daddy. This void impacts our children, our sons and daughters, you and me. Missing essential ingredients vital to our growth and development, follows us into adulthood and impacts the quality of our relationships. We struggle to build healthy, whole, and lasting relationships. Our marriages are weak because the individuals who come together are scared and broken, from the poor examples they had of relationships, marriage, and family. Even when they desire to live a life unlike what they saw and experienced, the toxicity experienced in their formative years makes it difficult to break the generational curse.

Reflections: Abandonment and Sense of Rejection

The Early Years - Trauma Phase 1

I was born and lived in Trinidad and Tobago until I was seven years old. My mom left my sister and I when I was about two years old to come to America. I would not meet her again until I was 7 years old. My memory of this time is hunger and fear. I do not have a memory of a loving, nurturing environment. "Mean" is the word I would use to describe my paternal grandmother who was entrusted to take care of my sister and I. I remember my mother would occassionally send a barrel filled with food and other items to us in Trinidad, but we were never allowed to touch. The empty feeling of hunger stirring in my stomach was my norm. I remember eating tomatoes with salt, or mangoes that I picked or had fallen from a tree. My sister and cousin cooked green bananas outside on the fire in a tin pot. We ate the cooked bananas with sprinkled salt for flavor. I was so skinny, my aunt who came to visit from America described me as "one of those starving African children." Her report to my mom on our condition prompted my mother to more aggressively pursue the process to get her children to the U.S.A. Reflecting upon my time spent in Trinidad, I do not have a vivid memory of any time or relationship with my dad. He did not live with us. He lived on the worksite where he was employed. He came around I think, which I say because I do not have a vivid, not even a dim memory of our interaction or a sense of his presence.

If he was physically present, he was emotionally unavailable. I pressed my memory continuously in deep search for a father/daughter memory. A caring/nurturing/loving or happy memory; a sense of safety and protection memory? Unfortunately, I found none.

Where were you Daddy? Why did you not take care of us? It was later in life I learned that my dad did not make it past 3rd or 4th grade. I am not clear on the levels of exposure, training or example he may have experienced that could have prepared him to assume the role of a father. It is my belief that he did not have the tools to operate in his role. This is the reality for so many men who are struggling to meet a standard, fulfill an expectation, be the father, and the superhero that their family can be proud of. Many are doing the best they can. Sadly however, they fall short resulting in emotional turmoil bred by failure. Frustrated, they retreat, bail, leave, abandoning their children, and their families. Some men stay and try, but harbor anger, frustration, disappointment, and feelings of inadequacy. Despite being unclear about their role in the family, they perform the best they can.

My question: Who is training men or boys as they grow, how to thrive in their role as a father/ daddy?

My mom sent for us and we left Trinidad to come to America. It was during this time of transition, that I learned I had an older sister who was living right there in Trinidad whom I had not known. I would also come to learn that I had a younger sister. My mom had divorced my dad and remarried and had a daughter. She had a whole other family in America. In the winter of 1974, scared and excited at the same time I exited the plane in New York and passed my mom in the airport. I did not know her. However, I would get to know this beautiful, tall statuesque model-like woman, who was strong. Being the eldest of 7 children, she loved family. She fought for and sought to protect them. My mom was an awesome cook. Her house was where family came together for holiday gatherings. Sunday dinners were a full spread, resembling a mini Thanksgiving feast. One of my fondest childhood memories was one beautiful Sunday in the summer, when my mom prepared dinner. She was about to set the table with all the Pyrex dishes of wonderful smelling food, but instead she decided to take dinner to the park. At the park, she laid out the food, we played stick ball with a branch of a tree we found. It was a fabulous day of fun and laughter. That day became one of my fondest childhood memory that I hold on too tightly. A parenting example I cherish! She was the "go-to" for counsel and guidance. I had the opportunity to spend four years with her. During my early connection with my mom, food was a major focus for us. She urged me to eat, so I would not look so skinny. I began to embrace, welcome and look forward to eating. I felt my mom's love through her food. I gleaned so much from my mom during this time. She provided an example of devotion to family, a love for cooking and sharing love through food. I can recall the smell and taste of freshly baked bread with butter she made one late evening after coming home from several days in the hospital. She looked at my 3 sisters and I, "what do you want, how about homemade bread" We all said yes, with joy and anticipation in our eyes. Family and family time were important. Game time was so much fun, she loved playing Scrabble. A no-nonsense parent, she was firm yet fun. She was expressive-she did not mince her words, she said what she meant and meant what she said. She was impulsive, wise, powerful, confident, a fighter. My mother was a woman of elegance, grace, and poise, she loved to look good. I loved being in her presence. Sometimes, I can see the reflection of her in me. Oh, how I wished I had more time with her. Just as I was feeling settled in my new life my mom became ill.

For two years I watched her fight illness; Leukemia attacked her body. I prayed to God to heal her, save her, but at 35 she was gone. For years I remained angry at God for not answering my prayers. My little faith was gone. My anger toward God was compounded by the anger I felt towards my earthly father. Where were you Daddy? Did you forget about us? Were you thinking about me or ever wonder if we were ok?

The Formative Years - Trauma Phase 2

In my journey now, I have developed despite an unstable, dysfunctional family life; experiencing mental, emotional, sexual, and physical abuse compounded by an overall sense of loss, grief, and abandonment—the death of my mother at age 11 and the murder of my grandmother, who was mugged and shot in the head when I was 12 years old. She had stepped in to take care of my sisters and I after my mom died. Just as we were trying to pick up the pieces, our lives were shattered once again. Where do we go? What happens now? Why is this happening GOD?

To add insult to injury, the men standing in the void of the sacred love of a father, who were supposed to love and protect me, instead violated me and stripped me of my innocence. From 5th to 9th grade this emotionally broken child found refuge in school. I excelled academically, danced, and played in the band; advancing to first Clarinet. I even skipped a grade and went from 7th to 9th grade. I used school to escape from the pain, only to return to reality at the end of each school day. From 5th grade to this day, a classmate, Diane— who at one time made fun of this quiet, shy, reclusive, and awkward child grieving in pain would become my friend. Like sisters, we became inseparable and her family, a safe place for me. Her home became the place I would run to.

I began a downward spiral in my teen years. I was weak and vulnerable to peer influence. Full of anger, the bitterness of my life woke me up daily. The continued mental, emotional, physical and sexual abuses left me feeling stifled with no voice. Unable to advocate for myself. When I stepped outside I could breathe, and my anger had a place and opportunity to be released. I was aggressive and ready to fight, triggered easily by casual words like 'your mother', 'shorty', 'hey you' and 'nigger'. My responses were strong and my fist ready to make contact. My friends were like my family and I fought with and for them. I began drinking, sneaking liquor from the cabinet in the house, and loved drinking wine coolers (the "in" thing in the 80's). It was like sipping on Kool-Aid. I would cut school and ride the train or bus for hours. At some point, I was truant from school for over 3 months, popping in on occasion taking tests and barely getting by.

Throughout this time, I bounced around from house to house where I would be reminded of the burden my presence added. Scared to open the fridge or keep the lights on to read as I would often hear, "you running up the light bill". I remember one day, I was working at KFC–Kentucky Fried Chicken, (my routine was usually school/ work/school or home). My co-workers invited me to join them at the movies. My supervisor allowed me to leave early and we went to a movie theater that was two blocks away from our job.

Once I got home, my aunt locked me out saying I wasn't following her rules and should find somewhere else to sleep. Once again, I can be thankful for the strangers whom God had placed in my life, they became lifetime friends. I had previously started a friendship with a schoolmate who lived in the projects nearby and she explained the situation to her mother, who allowed me to spend the night. Her mom contacted my aunt to let her know where I was, to which my aunt responded that she did not care and hung up the phone on her. The following day after calling my aunt repeatedly, she finally got to speak to her husband who told her to tell me to "come on home" that "we would work things out." I got there only to be confronted by a stream of derogatory words and blows to my body. My aunt's husband who was a 6 ft 11, semi-muscular man, grabbed me by my collar, and pinned me on the bed while my aunt sat and watched in close distance; him on top of me, smacking my face back and forth with his knees pressing on my chest and into my throat. He kept repeating with each blow, "you will follow the rules no matter what". Gasping for air and bawling in pain, I managed to utter "NO", so he grabbed me by my collar, threw me halfway across the room, and said "You have five minutes to pack your shit and leave." I found myself on the street with nowhere to go. I called a few people—family and friends—all with no positive response.

I finally reached out to my friend, Felicia, whose mother had allowed me to spend the night at their apartment the night before. I shared with her what had transpired, she urged me to come back. She allowed me to stay with them, which I did for several months. Though homelessness was my reality, I did not fully acknowledge that label until later in life. I was sitting in a meeting and heard how homeless students were described when it hit me that I was one of them.

Now driven by an unspoken longing and desire for love, safety, and care I hooked up with a boy, no, a young man (as he was in his early twenties), who became my 'boyfriend'. He said he cared about me and loved me. He brought me stuff, stuff I needed and stuff I wanted: clothing, jewelry, food, and gave me money. Some may label him a sugar daddy, a term I was unfamiliar with at the time. All I knew was that I was getting some stuff and finally got the attention that I wanted and was desperately longing for,. But at what cost? I soon realized that I had found myself in a controlling, abusive relationship, that I had to get out of. Stalked, he would call my job at the KFC as soon as I clocked in to work, to describe how I was dressed or how my hair looked. He met me outside as I was leaving work one night and held a gun to my head, stating "if 'he' could not have me, then no one else would," he threatened. Thank God that the manager of the restaurant came out and persuaded him to walk away. A few days later he attacked me in the stairwell of the projects where I had been staying with my friend. He grabbed me, threw me down a flight of stairs, ripped the chain he had bought me from my neck, punched and slapped me, and then left.

God in the Midst–He Uses Earthly Vessels

The flip side to this was, as all this was occuring, I decided to refocus on my education. I earnestly wanted to graduate high school. I did not want to embody the words which were spoken over me by relatives, "you will be a high school dropout, pregnant, on the street, and won't amount to anything". I needed to prove them wrong. I connected with a Guidance Counselor, who I will refer to as Mrs. H. As I reflect she was one of the many angels (persons) that God used in my life. It was with her, the first time that I can remember communicating with someone at school the depth of what was going on in my life. She provided counsel and guidance. She connected me with resources and opened doors of opportunities that I could never have imagined. I became active in school again. She helped me get back on track and showed me that college was a possibility for me. Mrs. H made me believe that I did not have to just go to community college, I could attend a university. Through her guidance and support, and the encouragement from other staff and teachers I applied for the Higher Educational Opportunity Program [HEOP]. It was a scholarship opportunity that provided academic support and financial assistance to young people who may not have met all the admissions criteria for traditional college, but showed promise of succeeding in college. Little did I know, that I would be one of over 300 students, vying for the opportunity to be selected for one of the 40 slots that were available. After several rounds of interviews and screenings the group size kept getting smaller, and I was still there. To my amazement, several weeks went by and one day I received a letter in the mail; "Congratulations - YOU HAVE BEEN ACCEPTED!"

I partook in all the senior excitement and activities; participated in the yearbook committe, attended the senior trip and prom all decked out (partially benefiting from a fashion show I modeled in and was able to keep the dress at a super discount). At this stage in my life, I finally found myself in a healthy, growth facilitating and supportive relationship. LB was my boyfriend. He was disciplined, athletic, strong, and loving. His sister was my best friend, we had been in the same fifth grade class and built a friendship that I still treasure today. Another divine connection, her family treated and loved me as if I was one of their own. They are a major part of my grounding and consistency; God has blessed me with a family to fill the void of my own.

On the day of my high school graduation, I was given special recognition, and sat on stage amongst the other highly accomplished students. I was awarded a small financial scholarship to support books and academic supplies. On this special day, there were no blood family members of mine present. I did however have two special people [angels] who have remained a constant in my life. My best friend, 'Diane' and the man who would show me what it meant to be loved, 'LB'. He cared and took care of me in the manner that I would have expected a father/family member to look out for me. I was always thankful for their presence in my life, but I did not know to acknowledge God at the time for the gift they were to me.

The Turning Point- Finding My Voice

I entered college summer of 1986. The scholarship program required for me to participate in a summer enrichment experience which was designed to prepare us for the collegiate journey.

My experience at this major private university was a turning point for me. The summer experience provided counseling, academic enrichment and support, self-esteem, and self-development through the teaching of history and culture. I gained exposure to accomplished people, facilitated by caring and supportive staff who believed in our promise, possibilities, and potential.

Where void, lack, or the absence of supportive family exists, God uses his earthly agents—angels that dwell amongst us—to serve on His behalf. One of those earthly agents was this awesome man 'LB' who supported and believed in me. He ensured that I always had what I needed, everything from a small refrigerator for my dorm room, food, and even quarters to do my laundry. He looked out constantly and even bought me a car that he fixed up, painted, and fully decked out, so that I was able to get around.

My collegiate experience was a serious eye-opening part of my journey. I began that Fall still somewhat quiet and reserved, but I harnessed a growing inner confidence. My life was turning around. A resident in the dorm room of a major university. For the next four years, the campus became my primary home, leaving only on occasions to spend time with friends who had become my surrogate family. Thanks to the NOAH Program, and the dynamic staff under the leadership of Dean Frank W. Smith, I was exposed to people of noble character and intellect who believed in us and our potential.

We were privileged to sit at the feet of giants, such as Dr. Josef Ben-

Jochannan, Ivan Van Sertima, John Henry Clarke, Gil Noble, Regent Adelaide Sandford, (to name a few) who had spent years studying, researching and teaching the history of people of color. My eyes were opened to the richness of my history. I was introduced to a book which would profoundly impact my thinking, There Is a River: The Black Struggle for Freedom in America by Vincent Harding. This book opened a portal of awareness and insight to the history and resilient spirit of black people from their origins in Africa to freedom at the end of the Civil War. It was during my collegiate experience that my self-awareness grew and I began to believe that I was a gift, talented, uniquely created and from a lineage of strong people who overcame many obstacles, even more traumatic than mine. They were survivors. They did not just survive, they thrived against the odds and with less opportunity and resources than were available to me. If they could do it, if they could find their voices and make an impact, so could I. I was deeply inspired and so I became fierce, vocal, and intense. They even nicknamed me "militant midget".

I was elected into a student leadership role as President. We lead boycotts and organized marches in solidarity with the people of South Africa seeking freedom from apartheid, The Sullivan Principles underpinned our objectives (I would later learn the value of this and all the various experiences I encountered along my life's journey). I was short in stature, but strong, bold, and full of life, creativity, and a deep desire to expose others to my heightened awareness. I wanted to help others find their voices, see their worth, and believe for the possibility a better life. This led me to become an activist and a voice for our youth; a path that I have remained on for the past 27 years.

I entered college with limited career guidance seeking to pursue a career as a Systems Analyst which seemed to be a lucrative option. I I emerged from my collegiate experience with a different career path– Liberal Arts –with a focus on English, History & Speech Communication Arts. With bold confidence, I can now stand before anyone and hold my ground. I was a force to be reckoned with. In the wordsof William Shakespeare "and though she be but little, she is fierce"

I started out as a volunteer Career Counselor with a community-based organization serving "at-risk youth". It was in this space that I found my passion. I found vessels like me who were struggling to deal with life issues and figure out their way.

A 27 year career in reflection, has afforded me the opportunity to serve and elevate the lives of thousands of youth and their families, who like me, did not have a smooth road to travel. They too were ill equipped for the journey and faced insurmountable obstacles, detours and pitfalls along the way. Yet, they continued to travel. I am them, they are me. We are awalking reflections of hardship and resilience. I am thankful for the revelation of God's presence in my life. I have been covered by the invisible yet warm blanket of God's grace.

As I reflect on this chapter of my life, I now recognize the favor of God. Imagine what our lives would be like if we paused often and reflected on not just the pain of the journey but the totality of the experiences. How we replay our story. I did not die on the journey. What did not kill me made me stronger. I am here despite the evil acts of others. He covered me.

I acknowledge, and I am thankful for the people, places and circumstances God placed in my life. I am the product of all my experiences, both good and bad. I have found that with God, and a decision to be intentional in developing a relationship with Jesus Christ I found the healing needed, a blueprint to follow, and an open arm full of love, compassion, forgiveness, hope, favor, grace, mercy, acceptance, and safety.

A comforter, supporter, and friend; a daddy, who promised to never leave or forsake me. We learn of Him through His Word–The Bible. We begin to know Him by His actions. It is this relationship that took me to another level. I was elevated to a place where my confidence was drawn from the self-awareness of my cultural history, and the newfound and growing knowledge of the One who created me. This divine internal union of knowledge and wisdom began reshaping the view I held of myself.

I am a special and beloved daughter in the eyes of my Father. The Orchestrator, the Creator of all things, who knew me before the foundation of the earth and predestined me and my path. This revelation and growing relationship cultivated in me a more holistic viewpoint and acceptance of myself.

Viewing my life through this new lens, the story I had been replaying for years was reshaping. My position in the story began to shift the more I acknowledged the presence of God, my Heavenly Father, in the midst of my story. As my connection to my Heavenly Father grew, a new understanding and growing compassion for my earthly father began to emerge.

Sources Cited:

1. The National Fatherhood Initiative (2017. U.S. Census Bureau. Data represent children living without a biological, step, or adoptive father.)

Allowing Myself to be LIFTED UP

Chapter 2: Who's Your Daddy?

Looking Back, as you reflect on your developmental years, can you identify the divine connections/relationships, earthly angels and the people who have impacted your life? Can you see the blessings amid your pain?

_____
_____
_____
_____
_____
_____
_____
_____
_____
_____
_____
_____
_____
_____
_____
_____
_____
_____
_____
_____
_____
_____
_____
_____
_____
_____
_____
_____
_____

MY DECLARATION:

- ✓ There is more to my story - I can recognize the positive and negative experiences and see how they helped shape who and how I am.

- ✓ Healing is available to me. I have a blueprint to follow and open arms full of love, compassion, hope, grace, mercy, acceptance and safety.

CHAPTER 3

Learning to Love Me

My only childhood memory of my dad is quite faint, almost non-existent. Having no solid memory of any connection with him during my early years while growing up in Trinidad, I have sat for countless hours, days, weeks and pondered for years in search of a memory that I can grab hold of which would help me frame a reference to anything about him.

From up until the age of twelve or thirteen, I had been told by family members that my daddy was dead. Throughout my teen years and into adulthood, if anyone asked about my parents I would say that they were both deceased.

Throughout those years, the only thing I had of my dad was a small 3x5 black and white wallet photo. Written on the back was a short message. One that I did not fully internalize until much later in life. A grown adult, now 50 years old, it was like I was viewing this picture and reading his message to me for the very first time. As I read his message, I wondered when had it been written? Who gave it to me? I am not even sure how long I have had it for.

The words written on the back of the photo would give me a deep sense of comfort, and while I could not recall my dad ever telling me he loved me, there it was, "Hi Arlene, my love for you is still in my heart for you". In this warm friendly greeting he declared that there was indeed a place in his heart for me. He called himself, "your loving Daddy". Short words that I grabbed hold of and cherished. His physical presence a void. His emotional presence weak, faint. In this short but powerful message, I was touched with gratitude, for the words written seemed to come from a deep and loving place. He repeats the words, "Be good to yourself: ok, ok" twice, as in emphasis. There was a genuine concern for my self-care. That I'd be ok. He let me know that because he loved me, he wanted me to take care of myself. He gave me an assignment. Knowing that he was not there to do it, he provided instruction and guidance. The value and importance of self-care is admonished by many, but we seldom give it the focus and attention necessary. I am instructed to care for me. This is a message, an instruction/assignment I pass on to you. Yes you, reading this book.

For years, and to be truly transparent, for most of my life, I had not put myself first, despite being an avid believer in self-care and self-preservation, and yet I had given more of myself to the point of depletion; overcompensating for the desired validation of my worthiness. Can others see me and my value? Not trusting that they could, as I believed that my daddy must not have, because if he did, he would have moved heaven and earth to ensure my safety and affirm me through his actions.

I charge you and me to value our health and well-being, and make taking care of our physical, mental, emotional and spiritual wellness a priority. No one else can do this for us. It is a decision we must practice daily. Throughout my life and especially in my adulthood, I have struggled with self-care. I teach it, know the importance of it and wholeheartedly believe in it. For a long time I could not understand why if I know better, am I not doing better? I focused and cared for the needs of others, the youth and families I served, my job and especially my daughter but I neglected myself and my needs. Over the last few years of self-reflection, introspection, revelation, impartation and healing I have learned to embrace me more. I love on me more and focus on giving myself what I want and need.

He imparted in me wisdom and faith. "God is love". Long before I ever developed a knowledge of and relationship with God, my dad let me know that God is love and the word is emphasized by two markings beneath. What an awesome message to impart to your child.

My earthly daddy loved me and he let me know that my heavenly daddy is the embodiment of love, the greatest example. Then, he closed his message by signing his name, "micHeal". The analytical depth of this short message written on the back of my dad's picture has grown to hold such meaning for me. So much said in such short words. "Heal" I do not know if this was intentional but it was a message I received, internalized, and now share. This is my desire for all of us who have been disappointed, wounded, scared and hurt from not experiencing daddy the way we would have liked or felt we deserved. Our earthly daddy may not have been what we expected, but I welcome you on this journey of healing and forgiveness that frees us to live fully in our present and embrace a future of possibilities. It starts with a decision and a desire to release the weight of pain, disappointment, and unforgiveness to embrace and feel lightness birth out of compassion as we understand the agape love that our heavenly daddy has left as an example for us. The journey to my healing was only just beginning.

In the Spring of 2014, I received a strange message on Facebook, "Are you my cousin?" Non-trusting and suspicious of social media, I concluded it was spam or phishing and I ignored it. I then received another message, "Are you my cousin?" Sharing details that only a relative or someone in my family would know as it is not public information anywhere. I responded, and as I exchanged communication with this stranger over the internet, who was indeed my cousin; a door was opened that would take me on a surprising journey.

I was surprised to learn that I actually had family members who were looking for me and had been wondering what happened to my sister and I, as she noted in her message. This was the cousin, who grew with us during my early years in Trinidad. It was in this communication that I received the most startling piece of information. She started telling me about members of my family and said, "Your dad is doing ok, but having some health issues." WHAT? WHO? My DAD? What was she talking about? I had spent close to 40 years of my life believing that my dad was dead, because of what I had been told. This connection with my cousin opened doors that were closed. Doors that I didn't even know existed. A few months later one of my aunts [my mom's sister] went to Trinidad and actually connected with my dad and sent me pictures. She shared with me that my dad never stopped thinking about his children and that he did not know where or how to find us after my mother passed. He always hoped that one day he would see his children. So I shifted from not having any living parents to learning that my dad was alive and was living a life hopeful to connect with his children. WOW!

I soon had the opportunity to speak with my dad. A man of few words, he addressed me with an oh so thankful voice. I could not believe this was happening to me… it was surreal… Here I was actually speaking to my father. When did I last hear his voice? I could not recall. My daughter, was so happy to know that her grandfather was alive. Over the years, she had always asked me, "when are we going to visit your island?" Now she said, "when are we going to visit your dad?", Would she get to meet her grandfather? I remember an encounter I once had with a minister at church one Sunday on the subject of family. During our conversation, I remember sharing with Minister Brown that I had no desire to reconnect with family. While I had forgiven them—specifically my mom's side of the family for how they treated me. I did not see any value in connecting with them or establish a relationship. They were non-existent to me. He appealed to me, saying it was "important that I make a connection and it is essential to my healing and God's plan for my life". I resisted his message, which would later come back to my remembrance as I faced this new opportunity.

Not only did I connect with my dad's family, I connected to my mom's sister. Having visited with my dad in Trinidad, my aunt was excited about the opportunity to speak with me. I had been closed off to family interaction for over 30 years.

Wow, what a refreshing and healing encounter it was. We spoke for over 3 hours. I witnessed the hand of God working within me over the years. I was able to engage with each person I was reconnecting to <u>with peace</u> and <u>in peace</u>, with no anger or bitterness. I felt free in my communication, and felt no apprehensions in my expression. I was experiencing what true release and forgiveness felt like. So often we say we forgive, we are walking in forgiveness, and although we released and let go of the pain, it's not until we are confronted, or in the position to be tested, that we know where we truly stand.

Prior to this new revelation, I had no desire or interest to go to Trinidad since I had no awareness or connection to family there. Now things had changed. I spoke to and connected to my dad's two brothers—one living in Trinidad, the other living in New York—and his older sister living in Maryland. Through these conversations, I learned about my family, filled the gaps, and recognized how many voids actually existed in my life. I stepped into a new realm of awareness. Through ongoing communication with my cousin, my dad, and this new and developing connection with my family, I made the decision, I was going to Trinidad to reconnect with family. In December of 2014, my daughter and I embarked on a two-week trip to Trinidad, celebrating Christmas and New Years with our new-found family.

I was going to see my dad! In preparation for our trip I created a hardcover, bound, and printed full color photo book, which captured my life in pictures. I brought some clothing and other care items that I knew would be difficult to acquire. In the brief conversations with my dad, he said he too was preparing for my arrival. We booked a hotel as we were cautious as to what the experience would be.

After 40 years, there I was landing in and touching the soil of Trinidad and Tobago. My dad, cousin, and other family members were there to pick us up. It was a surreal experience. They were all strangers to me, but they were family and they were welcoming me back to my homeland. There I was embracing my dad. I couldn't believe this was happening. I would learn that my dad did not smile easily. He had lost the woman whom he had a long-term relationship with due to illness.

In my observation, I would say he might have been suffering from depression. He had challenges as a result of being an insulin dependent diabetic, lacked friendships, hobbies, outside involvements or affiliations, and appeared to be somewhat of a loner. I don't fully know what his emotional journey was during this experience. I can only speculate that, like me, he felt somewhat awkward, uncertain of how to interact with me, what to say and what not to say. Feeling a sense of loss, (he last saw me when I was about 7 years old), his baby girl was all grown up and introducing him to his granddaughter. All I knew was, there we were. He finally had me in his presence, and in my assessment, he missed the opportunity to say whatever was on his mind or in his heart. We cannot afford to miss sacred opportunities like these to reconnect and be fully transparent in sharing our feelings with others. We tend to hold back so much, not being fully present with those we care about, believing that we have other opportunities to share our feelings. We have to seize the moments, live and embrace them. A wonderful relationship has now been developed with my uncle Chris, who I speak to frequently who sends me encouraging text messages weekly.

Tomorrow is not promised. We should honor the gift of today and show the love and compassion of Christ. It was only through God's love that I stood in a place capable to embrace my daddy.

Brethren, I count not myself to have apprehended: but this one thing I do, forgetting those things which are behind, and reaching forth unto those things which are before, I press toward the mark for the prize of the high calling of God in Christ Jesus.

Philippians 3:13-14 KJV

Allowing Myself to be LIFTED UP

Chapter 3: Learning to Love Me

NOW... I am open to experience the power of forgiveness, reconciliation, and second chances. Who can I decide to forgive and seek to connect with if reconciliation was possible? Describe the present-day opportunities you can seize hold of to create the relationships your desire.

_____
_____
_____
_____
_____
_____
_____
_____
_____
_____
_____
_____
_____
_____
_____
_____
_____
_____
_____
_____
_____
_____
_____
_____
_____
_____
_____
_____
_____
_____

MY DECLARATION:

- ✓ I want to move forward in my life and be free. I release the hurt and fear and will no longer entertain old pains. I choose to honor the gift of today and release the narrative of yesterday to allow myself to live fully in my present.

CHAPTER 4

The Path Towards Healing

For so long I wondered what it would be like to have my father ever present in my life. This experience, this reconnection brought revelation to me. It was a time of true acknowledgment that my Heavenly Father had been with me, nurturing, guiding, loving, protecting and providing for me. My father, the one who gave seed, my earthly father is like an empty shell. I searched for substance, but didn't find it. I did not feel the love that I was hoping for. No wisdom or insight to bestow upon me. Connecting with him helped me to realize that he was unable to provide me what I needed, in the way I needed it. Over the next few days of my visit in Trinidad, I began questioning what I was feeling. I did not feel a strong stir of emotions. Instead a numbness had come over me and I oddly felt no real connection to the one with whom I sought connection from the most.

It was a true time of acknowledgment that my Heavenly Father had placed earthly vessels to watch over me. In particular, my daughter's father, a man who had known me since the age of 11 and connected with me later in my teenage years. He has kept watch over us faithfully, lovingly, and with great consistency. Even as our lives took different directions, we made a commitment to co-parent, and keep him fully active and engaged in every aspect of his daughter's life. I parented while single, but I was never a single parent. He was and is a fully active and engaged father. I also developed a strong support system that played a pivotal role in my daughter's' life. I was intentional about nurturing and preserving, as much as possible a strong bond between them. I never wanted my daughter to feel the void of an absentee father. While it has not been easy for any of us, what my daughter knows for sure is that her dad has always been there for her. She can count on him. Throughout her life she has spoken to him almost every day. Even though we live in different states, we were intentional in making sure that he saw her and spent time with her. I often share in my workshops with parents, "the issues that we fail to address within ourselves ferment in the lives of our children." How we show up, whether conscious or unconscious of our issues, and how they manifest in our daily actions has a distinct impact on the development of our children. I was determined to provide a better childhood experience for my daughter than mine. Yet, despite all my efforts, some of my scars and brokenness still impacted her, as she has experienced the void of broken families and the lack of presence and connection. My daughter so often would ask me about my family and I had very little to share with her.

I am thankful for the opportunity that God provided for me to meet my father even though it did not meet my expectations. I see that it was a necessary part of my journey.

Our meeting answered a barrage of questions and satisfied a longing that I had for so many years. I was looking and yearning for that feeling of genuine affection and love from my father. Our interaction was OK, and somewhat awkward, but I did not feel that from my dad. Instead, I felt a greater sense of connection with my uncle. It was in meeting him that I realized that the only faint memory I had of my dad was actually a memory of my uncle Stalin holding my hand. So, I remain with no memory of my dad's care or nurturing of me. I would learn that I have two younger sisters and had the opportunity to meet them. In connecting with them I realized that they had their dad physically present in their lives however, their relationship was weak, fragmented, and dysfunctional. They did not even call him daddy but referred to him by his first name.

I questioned, what did he do to prepare for my coming? He did not even offer a glass of water to quench my thirst. Instead, the questions lingered in my head: can you tell me anything about my childhood? Can you fill in the gaps about what happened between you and my mom? Did you know we were experiencing suffering and abuse at the hands of your mother and others? You said you never gave up hope that one day you would see your children, but what actions did you take to make that possible? These stirring questions were not coming from a place of anger or bitterness, but from disappointment. It was during this time and on this trip that I was able to release the emotions of failed expectations. I was able to acknowledge that my standards and expectations were real, basic, and realistic. However, a person cannot give what they do not have. So, I am able to accept you for who you are, where you are in your life, and I release, exhale, and stand in the place of thankfulness that I was given the opportunity to reconnect with my earthly father.

What God revealed to me in this experience was an understanding and acknowledgment that my desire for a relationship with my father, my need to fill the void of the absence of that relationship and the expectations that I have of a father are fundamental. In the absence of my earthly father my Heavenly Father has provided what I needed. He stands as the Example and I have truly experienced His love. I had an awesome encounter with God during this trip.

I truly believe in journaling. I have found it tremendously therapeutic. It is my place of reflection, release and revelation. Through journaling, I have had the opportunity to capture my God encounters. During these times I experienced a conversation with my Heavenly Father. You hear two voices in this dialogue. Me seeking clarity and revelation through questions and my Heavenly Father's responses to me.

"Dear Arlene, live! I have come so you have life. My instructions were, I set before you life and death, choose life choose to live." What does that mean? What does that look like? How do I do that? What are the actions, the decisions that I must make daily to experience this?

Living is an action word, it means that there is something I must do No one else can do it for me. I must care for my physical well-being. I must cultivate a joyful spirit.

"Create sacred spaces in your life. It is non-negotiable prayer, meditation, journaling, quiet, be still and listen to My voice. My joy, My peace cannot come from people, places, or situations. This must come from within. Do not leave your joy in the hands of others. Reclaim your authority, for I have given it to you. You know you better than anyone else. Do not expect people to read your mind. If you wanted things a certain way then do it, organize it, implement it, move it, create it, I have given the vision to you Arlene. I poured out My spirit to you. I revealed Myself to you. I have ordained you. I have predestined you. No one else can do for you what I have commanded you to do for you and the world. Don't commit to anyone or anything else until you can first commit to Me. When you commit to yourself, you are committing to Me. I am that I am that is in you. I created you. I flow through you. I am ever present with you. You have just failed to tap into me, and yourself. I have given you everything you need. Why do you continue to seek confirmation from the outside that I have blessed you? You are a walking example of My love, grace and mercy. You are complete. When I made you, I gave you everything you needed for your divine assignment, to fulfill your purpose, your promise, your possibilities. Invest time each day to reconnect with Me and allow Me to help you see yourself as I see you; divinely perfect. I poured out My power into you. You carry My anointing. I have gifted you. I certify you. I give you authority. I call you to arise my daughter and lead yourself first, let your life exemplify My light. You shine brightly, you glow, illuminating as you walk. Allow Me, My child to lead you and guide you along life's way. I will not let you stray but divinely allow all things to work together for your good, for you placed your full trust in Me. When I speak you listen to My instructions and you move accordingly without resistance. You follow through and allow my wisdom to be your guide. Seeking My counsel by learning how to focus on My voice, My guidance and drown out the distractions. Beware and remove those things, people, places and circumstances that stand in between us, in between you and fulfilling the divine assignment I have placed on your life. Rise up author, woman of words and spirit, speak to the masses and let them know thus said the Lord. Be My voice, let the message I have given you arise. Speak up, stop hiding in the shadows. Focus on what I have commanded you to do. Speak only life not negative defeated words. Affirm proclaim! Mind your words Arlene. You are a leader Acknowledge it! You

are a manager of time, money, resources, people, you are the driver of action! You can do anything just focus and commit to it. Let your actions speak."

During this encounter, the Lord spoke to my vulnerability and the void in my spirit... He helped me come home to myself "Arlene, give yourself the love you so greatly desire".

Issues: Vulnerability, Trust, Self-Concept, Self-Esteem,
Key Questions and Thoughts:

First, it is essential that we acknowledge where we are, living in the now, fully present, and grateful. We cannot turn back time. We embrace that time goes forward not backwards. We celebrate the fact that we are still here amongst the living. We welcome the opportunity each day provides

It is essential to build an understanding of how we show up in our day to day relationships; with our baggage, and with the experiences that shaped who we are. When we are honest with ourselves and hear the story; we replay, for some relive, and for many, hold on to like it was yesterday – in raw agony and bound with pain. We must ask ourselves "Am I showing up wounded, bruised, and broken?"

It is critical that as we seek to be in relationships with one another, that we seek to connect and dig deeper; moving beyond surface exchanges of "I love you" to reach a full understanding and acceptance of who a person is.

Looking at how we understand each other allows us to love more deeply. What is challenging for us, having this human experience is our ability to live the love that God has called us to live.

We struggle to be authentic, to be vulnerable to trust, and to acknowledge that we are human and we err. The practice of forgiveness is required.

DIGGING DEEPER:
Searching within the deeper thoughts in my head... I realize I struggle with thoughts and feelings of not being enough.

- I do not feel that I am valuable, important, and necessary.

41

The emotion that is often felt when daddy is absent is likened to a hole in the heart, mind, and spirit of an individual; who in turn questions their value, relevance, and significance to the world. They ask the question, "if my daddy, the person who contributed to giving me life did not see me worthy enough, did not love me enough, and wasn't committed to sticking around to raise me, and be a true father to me... what does that say about my worth or how much I am valued?"

There is a sense of jealousy and envy when we look around and see others with their daddies and admire their relationship and wonder why he stayed.

- How come their daddy is there?
- Where is my dad, did he not love me?
- Was I not worthy?
- Was I not beautiful?
- Did he not see or believe that I was special?

Oh, how I desired to have the experience of what many described as being a "Daddy's Girl". I wished I was fortunate enough to have experienced a relationship with my dad. I moved through life with shaky confidence, low self-concept, and feeling a void. The role that you would have played daddy—of loving and affirming; lifting me up, and helping me to know that I'm beautiful in your eyes; special, unique, a priceless treasure. I needed that affirmation from you!

There are so many questions, and thoughts that occupy my mind and sometimes are all consuming. I have come to realize that failure to engage in healthy dialogue about these thoughts, impact my ability to live well.

Not truly understanding who I am, I sought for and faced the burning desire and need for affirmation.

- Do I matter, am I lovable, am I enough?
- Am I special?
- Am I worthy of your time and attention?
- Can I trust you with my heart, hope, dreams, desires, fears, and insecurities?

- Can I count on you to be there for me, to love and support me, be the biggest cheerleader for me?
- Will you treat me with honor and respect?
- Will you cherish and adore me, treat me special and treasure me as though I am priceless?
- Can and/or will you protect me, mentally, physically, emotionally, spiritually?

<u>If we begin to look inward, we can ask ourselves:</u>

- Am I hoping for my relationships to fill this deeper void that only my Heavenly Father can fulfill?
- Do I feel equipped to be in relationship?
- Do I know how to give and receive love?
- Am I controlling, manipulative, self-serving, or self-sabotaging?

<u>How do we begin the healing process to strengthen our earthly and heavenly relationships?</u>

In order for the healing process to begin we first have to acknowledge that we are in pain, hurting, bruised, and broken. This requires us to be honest with ourselves. Spend some time in quiet reflection. Close friends, loved ones or significant others can be a source of support—their observation, their interaction (or as my daughter would say, "we need to spend some time on somebody's couch") —can help us to dig deep, process and unpack the baggage we are carrying.

We are often so focused on finding and building a relationship with someone else that we fail to invest the time to build a relationship with ourselves. Taking the time to connect and know yourself is essential.

We cannot truly be to others what we cannot first be to ourselves. We need a trusted support system. My greatest healing occurred for me during my faith walk. I am thankful that I have been grounded by biblically sound teaching which has brought great insight. I surrounded myself with solid people and developed strong relationships and friendships, which have proved truly beneficial on my journey.

Allowing Myself to be LIFTED UP

<u>Chapter 4: The Path Towards Healing</u>

Self-love... decide to unpack the misguided views of how you identify yourself. Make a list of what is important to you in a healthy relationship and be intentional about cultivating those qualities and experiences for yourself. Your circle of influence plays a pivotal role in your self-development. Are you around people who are - caring, honest, supportive and committed to growth?

_____
_____
_____
_____
_____
_____
_____
_____
_____
_____
_____
_____
_____
_____
_____
_____
_____
_____
_____
_____
_____
_____
_____
_____
_____
_____
_____
_____

MY DECLARATION:

- ✓ Today I _____, embrace the opportunity to care for and treat myself the way I would like others to treat me. I give myself the love I desire.

- ✓ I choose to surround myself with people who demonstrate unconditional love, they support my healing, growth and believe in my potential, possibilities and promise.

CHAPTER 5

Getting From Here to There

Our Heavenly Father embraces and finds joy in His children's love for Him. Love is an action. We demonstrate the love of God, when we, His children, sing His praises, believe in His goodness, trust in His promises, and allow His presence into our lives. This demonstrates that we have intimacy with Him. This is when God's loving attention is experienced.

There's something about a child who calls out to their Father. They are focused and clear about what they want. Their Heart's desire and intention,unshakable.

Look to the blueprint/the example and set your course on a path of discovering who God is to learn about your Heavenly Father. An everlasting, unchangeable example, we can learn about Him through His Word.

Getting to know Him – Our Heavenly Father

In the studies of God's Words through the scriptures found in our Bible, Jesus spoke fervently about His Father. It is noted that the central message and purpose of our Savior Jesus Christ was to restore us to a relationship with our daddy in Heaven.

These following scriptures can Help us to grow and build a relationship with our Heavenly Father that we may call Him Abba and to grow in intimacy with God.

When I read the Bible and learned about God through His Words, I learned about "Daddy Love" as reflected in His Word.

John 3:16 (ESV) —"For God so loved the world, that He gave His only Son, that whoever believes in Him should not perish but have eternal life".
Wow, the sacrifice of giving that which is most precious to you, your most priceless treasure, flesh of your flesh. What kind of love is that? It is a deep abiding love that we can experience as we seek to build a relationship with our Heavenly Father, our daddy.

Isaiah 64:8 —"But now, O Lord, thou art our Father; we are the clay, and thou our potter; and we all are the work of Thy hand.

Deuteronomy 32:10— "The Father carded him as the apple of His eye"

Psalm 68:5-6 (TLB)— "He is a Father to the Fatherless; He gives justice to the widows, for He is holy.[a] He gives families to the lonely, and releases prisoners from jail, singing with joy! But for rebels there is famine and distress."

Isaiah 9:6— "For unto us a child is born, unto us a son is given: and the government shall be upon His shoulder: and His name shall be called Wonderful, Counselor, The Mighty God, The Everlasting Father, The Prince of Peace."

Matthew 6:8— "Your Father knows what you need before you ask him"

Matthew 6:26— "Look at the birds of the air; they do not sow or reap or store away in bonds, and yet your Heavenly Father feeds them. Are you not much more valuable than day?"

Matthew 18:12-14— "What do you think? If a man owns 100 sheep, and one of them wanders away, will he not leave the 99 on the hills and go look for the one that wandered off? And if he finds it, I tell you the truth, he is happy about that one sheep than about the 99 that did not wander off. In the same way your Father in Heaven is not willing that any of these little ones should be lost."

Luke 6:35-36— "Being merciful just as your Father is merciful"

Luke 12:32— "Do not be afraid, little flock, for your Father has been pleased to give you the Kingdom"

John 14:1-2— "Do not let your Heart be troubled. Trust in God: trust also in me. In my Father's house are many rooms; if it were not so, I would've told you. I am going there to prepare a place for you."

John 16:27 — "No, the Father Himself loves you because you have loved me and have believed that I came from God."

Romans: 8:15-16— "For you did not receive a spirit that makes you a slave again to fear, but you received the Spirit of son-ship. And by Him we cry, Abba, Father. The Spirit Himself testifies with our spirit that we are God's children.

Matthew 7:9-11— "Oh which of you, if his son asked for bread, will give him a stone? Or if he asked for a fish, will give him a snake? If you, then, though you are evil, know how to give good gifts to your children, how much more will your Father in Heaven give good gifts to those who ask!"

1John 3:1 — "How great is the love the Father has lavished on us that we should be called children of God! And that is what we are!"

John 15:16 — "The Father will give you whatever you ask in Jesus name"

2 Corinthians 6:18 and 2 Samuel 7:14 —"I will be a Father to you and you will be my sons and daughters, says the Lord Almighty"

Ephesians 1:3-5— "Praise be to God and Father of our Lord Jesus Christ, who has blessed us in the Heavenly realms with every spiritual blessing in Christ. For He chose us... In love He predestined find us to be adopted as 'children' "

Ephesians 3:20-21— "Now to the Father who is able to do immensely more than all we ask or imagine, according to His power that is at work within us, to Him be glory in the church and in Christ Jesus throughout all generations, forever and ever!" Amen"

Recognize, acknowledge, declare and decree:

i.) The value, belief, and attitude adjustments needed for my transformational journey towards wholeness.

ii.) The love of God Heals: what I think about myself, how I see myself, how I see other people.

iii.) Develop an inner circle—Cultivate a healthy environment that fosters healing, deliverance, and growth.

iv.) Develop self-love. Develop your interpersonal relationship by monitoring your internal dialogue.

v.) Self-discovery: Get to know your source—God's intended purpose for you.

vi.) Develop your self-worth and strengthen your self-esteem, reclaim your value as you ingest His word.

vii.) Reframe your self-image and self-concept. Be intentional about how you care for yourself which is God's temple. Note that Jesus never spoke negatively of Himself.

viii.) Study God's Word and gain insight. This worthwhile investment in your self-development strengthens your foundation and clears a path for your journey of discovery, building your:

- Self Love
- Self-Confidence
- Self-Respect
- Self-Assertiveness
- Self-Motivation
- Self-Forgiveness
- Self-Affirmation

Become self-assured, walking in love and with a holy boldness knowing that:

- I am a child of God. But to all who have received Him—those who believe in His name—He has given the right to become God's children ... (John 1:12).
- I am a branch of the true vine, and a conduit of Christ's life. I am the

true vine and my Father is the gardener. I am the vine; you are the branches. The one who remains in me—and I in him—bears much fruit, because apart from me you can accomplish nothing (John 15:1, 5).

• I am a friend of Jesus. I no longer call you slaves, because the slave does not understand what his master is doing. But I have called you friends, because I have revealed to you everything I heard from my Father (John 15:15).

• I have been justified and redeemed. But they are justified freely by His grace through the redemption that is in Christ Jesus (Romans 3:24).

• My old self was crucified with Christ, and I am no longer a slave to sin. We know that our old man was crucified with Him so that the body of sin would no longer dominate us, so that we would no longer be enslaved to sin (Romans 6:6).

• I will not be condemned by God. There is therefore now no condemnation for those who are in Christ Jesus (Romans 8:1).

• I have been set free from the law of sin and death. For the law of the life-giving Spirit in Christ Jesus has set you free from the law of sin and death (Romans 8:2).

• As a child of God, I am a fellow heir with Christ. And if children, then heirs (namely, heirs of God and also fellow heirs with Christ)—if indeed we suffer with him so we may also be glorified with him (Romans 8:17).

• I have been accepted by Christ. Receive one another, then, just as Christ also received you, to God's glory (Romans 15:7).

• In Christ Jesus, I have wisdom, righteousness, sanctification, and redemption. He is the reason you have a relationship with Christ Jesus, who became for us wisdom from God, and righteousness and sanctification and redemption … (1 Corinthians 1:30).

• My body is a temple of the Holy Spirit who dwells in me. Do you not know that you are God's temple and that God's Spirit lives in you? (1 Corinthians 6:19)

• I am joined to the Lord and am one spirit with Him. But the one united with the Lord is one spirit with him (1 Corinthians 6:17).

• God leads me in the triumph and knowledge of Christ. But thanks be to God who always leads us in triumphal procession in Christ and who makes known through us the fragrance that consists of the knowledge of Him in every place (2 Corinthians 2:14).

- I am a new creature in Christ. So then, if anyone is in Christ, he is a new creation; what is old has passed away—look, what is new has come! (2 Corinthians 5:17)
- I have become the righteousness of God in Christ. God made the one who did not know sin to be sin for us, so that in Him we would become the righteousness of God. (2 Corinthians 5:21)
- I have been made one with all who are in Christ Jesus. There is neither Jew nor Greek, there is neither slave nor free, there is neither male nor female—for all of you are one in Christ Jesus (Galatians 3:28).
- I am no longer a slave, but a child and an heir. So you are no longer a slave but a son, and if you are a son, then you are also an heir through God (Galatians 4:7).
- I have been set free in Christ. For freedom Christ has set us free. Stand firm, then, and do not be subject again to the yoke of slavery (Galatians 5:1).
- I have been blessed with every spiritual blessing in the Heavenly places. Blessed is the God and Father of our Lord Jesus Christ, who has blessed us with every spiritual blessing in the Heavenly realms in Christ (Ephesians 1:3).
- I am chosen, holy, and blameless before God. For He chose us in Christ before the foundation of the world that we may be holy and unblemished in His sight in love (Ephesians 1:4).
- I am redeemed and forgiven by the grace of Christ. In Him we have redemption through His blood, the forgiveness of our trespasses, according to the riches of His grace (Ephesians 1:7).
- I have been predestined by God to obtain an inheritance. In Christ we too have been claimed as God's own possession, since we were predestined according to the one purpose of Him who accomplishes all things according to the counsel of His will (Ephesians 1:11).
- I have been sealed with the Holy Spirit of promise. And when you heard the word of truth (the gospel of your salvation)--when you believed in Christ--you were marked with the seal of the promised Holy Spirit

(Ephesians 1:13).

• Because of God's mercy and love, I have been made alive with Christ. But God, being rich in mercy, because of His great love with which He loved us, even though we were dead in transgressions, made us alive together with Christ—by grace you are saved! (Ephesians 2:4-5)

• I am seated in Heavenly places with Christ.... And He raised us up with Him and seated us with Him in the Heavenly realms in Christ Jesus ... (Ephesians 2:6).

• I am God's workmanship created to produce good works. For we are His workmanship, having been created in Christ Jesus for good works that God prepared beforehand so we may do them (Ephesians 2:10).

• I have been brought near to God by the blood of Christ. But now in Christ Jesus you who used to be far away have been brought near by the blood of Christ (Ephesians 2:13).

• I am a member of Christ's body and a partaker of His promise... The Gentiles are fellow heirs, fellow members of the body, and fellow partakers of the promise in Christ Jesus (Ephesians 3:6). (See also Ephesians 5:30.)

• I have boldness and confident access to God through faith in Christ... In whom we have boldness and confident access to God because of Christ's faithfulness (Ephesians 3:12).

• My new self is righteous and holy... Put on the new man who has been created in God's image--in righteousness and holiness that comes from truth (Ephesians 4:24).

• I was formerly darkness, but now I am light in the Lord... For you were at one time darkness, but now you are light in the Lord. Walk as children of the light (Ephesians 5:8).

• I am a citizen of Heaven. Our citizenship is in Heaven--and we also await a savior from there, the Lord Jesus Christ ... (Philippians 3:20).

• The peace of God guards my Heart and mind. And the peace of God that surpasses all understanding will guard your Hearts and minds in Christ Jesus (Philippians 4:7).

• God supplies all my needs. And my God will supply your every need according to His glorious riches in Christ Jesus (Philippians 4:19).

- I have been made complete in Christ.... You have been filled in Him, who is the head over every ruler and authority (Colossians 2:10).
- I have been raised up with Christ. Therefore, if you have been raised with Christ, keep seeking the things above, where Christ is, seated at the right hand of God (Colossians 3:1).
- My life is hidden with Christ in God. For you have died and your life is hidden with Christ in God (Colossians 3:3).
- Christ is my life, and I will be revealed with Him in glory. When Christ (who is your life) appears, then you too will be revealed in glory with Him (Colossians 3:4).
- I have been chosen of God, and I am holy and beloved. Therefore, as the elect of God, holy and dearly loved, clothe yourselves with a Heart of mercy, kindness, humility, gentleness, and patience... (Colossians 3:12).
- God loves me and has chosen me. We know, brothers and sisters loved by God, that He has chosen you... (1 Thessalonians 1:4).

The more we embrace the Word of God and study the truths from Scripture about who we are in Christ; we can stand assuredly on the foundation of His word. We are grateful for His love and compassion for us and we can walk in love and peace knowing that we are divinely created and loved by our Heavenly Father. As we grow in Him, we learn that he has forgiven us and we are worthy of His Love. It is now time to forgive ourselves.

This worship song has helped me,
"I Forgive Me"
Sung by James Fortune and FIYA, lyrics says:

Sometimes the hardest person for you to forgive
Is the one you see in the mirror everyday
It's time for you to get free
I've decided to stop replaying regrets
And I've decided to tell my past by
I cannot change what I did
But I did change what you gave
When you took my place
No more guilt but grace
Feel it all went too long
Watching reruns of my wrongs
Take the shame away
Reliving mistakes you wash away
I forgive me
I forgive me
I forgive me
I forgive me

Allowing Myself to be LIFTED UP

Chapter 5: Getting From Here to There

Changing the narrative—seeing myself as God sees me. Write your new song, declaration statement, poem or affirmation. Below, write 10 new positive statements of belief about yourself. Practice applying the power of the 'Tongue' and say it out loud so you can hear it.

_____
_____
_____
_____
_____
_____
_____
_____
_____
_____
_____
_____
_____
_____
_____
_____
_____
_____
_____
_____
_____
_____
_____
_____
_____
_____

MY DECLARATION:

- ✓ Today I _____, forgive myself for defining who I am based on my past experiences and using negative words to describe myself.

- ✓ I commit to choosing self-descriptive language that affirms me and reinforces the images of me as seen through Gods eyes.

CHAPTER 6

Can I Trust You?

There is a confidence in knowing He can carry you

For those of us who have experienced multiple levels of disappointment, heartbreak, betrayal and struggle with the void of an absentee or emotionally unavailable father; we often struggle in our ability to build, develop, establish, and maintain trust. The Bible states, "trust in the Lord with all your heart and lean not to your own understanding and in all your ways acknowledge Him and He will direct your path." -Proverbs 3:5-6.

Can I depend on you Go?, Can I really? Can I trust You to carry me? Can I truly walk out the faith I say I have? How is it that I can still ask these questions or even doubt your ability to carry me when you have proven yourself trustworthy throughout my life? You have been with me even when I was not consciously aware of your presence.

My relationship with God is not one that I started, but one that God started with me before the foundation of the earth. In order for our relationship to grow and flourish I have to engage and invite Him into my life. I had to call out to "ABBA Father God!"

As I pen this book, I am walking in another dimension in my relationship with God. I am confident that HE can carry me. I stand in full surrender with my hands up. Yes Daddy Lift Me Up! I acknowledge that You have been carrying me throughout my entire life. You have kept me, and I trust you.

I have found myself in the place where trusting and leaning on Him is not only necessary, but is also in alignment with his commandments, his instructions, and the voice of Holy Spirit within me. I am walking in obedience to God's calling on my life like never before.

I journal and when I reflect on my thoughts over the years, I have consistently prayed for the same areas of my life: Discipline, Obedience, Consistency, Follow through/Execution. I am walking out my prayer daily; as the Lord says to do, I do. When He says move, I move; stay, I stay; go, I go; execute, I execute. I am not wavering. I am not holding back. I am moving with a holy boldness, and with fervent persistence. There is this phenomenal feeling that I've been having over the past several months, that is evident in my walk, and my talk... my whole countenance has changed. When people see me they say they see a glow around me and I don't seem as stressed as before. When they say what is different about you? I answer, "this is what obedience looks like, I have rested and placed all my cares and concerns in the hands of the Lord. I walk in greater peace and joy, freedom, and contentment. I am watching and experiencing God, my Father, my daddy lift me up. He is not just at work, He is manifesting His glory in my life. He is opening doors that no man can shut. He is meeting me at my points of need. He is fostering divine connections. He is clearing a path and accelerating my growth and movement like never before. I stand in AWE of You God.

Strong and courageous I stand. As I recount, reflect and bask in the work of His hands in my life over the past few months:
- God's declaration and release from a job I loved, but was compromising my health and not allowing me time to be obedient to God's call on my life.
- After suffering for years with debilitating headaches, that sent me to the Emergency Room, I experienced God's healing power as He covered me during cranial & spinal surgery to help release the pressure and blockage of accumulated spinal fluid between my brain and spine.
- God continues to show me He is a provider. Meeting me at my point of need. He continues to establish divine connections, plac-

ing the right people in my path.
- Trust requires surrender, intimacy, and forgiveness, but what exactly is trust? Where do you obtain confidence and belief in someone, when all you've ever known is dissapointment? It is critical to hear what people say, but so much more to watch what they do.

Joshua 1:9 reminds me "have I not commanded you? Be strong and courageous. Do not be afraid; not be discouraged, for the Lord Your God will be with you wherever you go."

<u>Build trust with God and with man:</u>

Regardless of how hurt I may have been as a child, I had to rebuild my belief in people by allowing myself to be vulnerable to hurt again and to take the risk anyway. We can grow in trusting God and man by strengthening these areas:

1. Self-Awareness—Know yourself intimately and your intentions.
2. Character— Work on aligning your walk and talk.
3. Authenticity— Be honest and sincere about how you feel and why you feel that way.
4. Communicate openly— Give and receive feedback.

Remember that trust is built overtime, through demonstrated and consistent action.

Other Supporting Scriptures to help develop trust:
    Samuel 7:28 | Psalm 9:10 | Psalm 13:5 | Psalm 20:7

Allowing Myself to be LIFTED UP

Chapter 6: Can I Trust You?

I Choose to Trust. In deciding to build trust in others I am working on being trustworthy. Write 5 to 10 key actions that can strengthen your ability to trust yourself and others. Will you practice honest open communication? Will you say what you mean, and mean what you say? Will you commit to being authentic, transparent, and vulnerable? Will you be conscious in your decision making to ensure they align with your values and beliefs in developing healthy relationship with yourself and others?

___
___
___
___
___
___
___
___
___
___
___
___
___
___
___
___
___
___
___
___
___
___
___
___
___
___
___
___
___
___
___

MY DECLARATION:

- ✓ I commit to learning to trust myself and developing a trustworthy spirit.

- ✓ I am learning to trust God to lift me up!

CHAPTER 7

Calling Out to Him

Seek Revelation of Him, of your father, evidence of His desire to interact, because of his prevailing love.

My Father reveals and I am inspired. The evidence of His presence in my life is that you see me illuminated. I am a child of the Most High God. He is my daddy. He created me and blew the breath of life into me. He calls me His own. He said he would never leave me or forsake me and that He will be with me always. So, when trials and tribulations or situations come I can call out to Him.

He loves me, He loves us. He loves His children. He loves His creation. How do we get God's attention? We must seek Him. As our lives... and our prayers... are focused on seeking God's Kingdom first, above all other desires, then we get God's attention and when we get His attention, He promises He will give us what we need.

"Seek ye first the Kingdom of God, and His righteousness; and all these things shall be added unto you." Matthew 6:33

In order to go about getting daddy's attention, we have to call Him by His name. We have to speak to Him in a voice that He can hear.

The adoration that earthly fathers extend to their children is experienced through his consistent action. His demonstration of love. It is in what he does and what he says about us and to us. It is experienced in his affirmation, protection, provision, prayer and covering over his family. It is found in his care and compassion as well as his firm correction and discipline necessary to provide sound guidance and structure to our lives. He stands as an example for and to us. We find peace and safety, comfort and joy, in his presence and when his spirit is around. When a father loves and adores his children and his children extend the same love and joy in return, a healthy relationship is formed. Trust is established, and you have an unshakable confidence in him. It is this confidence and belief in who he is to us and how we feel in his presence that allows us to feel safe in asking – "Daddy lift me up?"

Intimacy requires full and complete surrender. It requires vulnerability. It can only be established through the building of healthy relationships. It requires an investment of time and is develops over time.

Dictionary.com defines Intimacy as:
- "a close, familiar, and usually affectionate or loving personal relationship with another person or group.
- a close association with or detailed knowledge or deep understanding of a place, subject, period of history, etc.:
- an act or expression, serving as a token of familiarity, affection, or the like: to allow the intimacy of using first names.
- an amorously familiar act; liberty.
- sexual intercourse. [NOT APPLICABLE TO THIS BOOK REFERENCE AND USE OF THE WORD]
- the quality of being comfortable, warm, or familiar

<u>Some synonyms for intimacy are</u>: closeness, togetherness, affinity, rapport, attachment, familiarity, friendliness, friendship, amity, affection, warmth, confidence.

In order for intimacy to occur, a relationship must first be established. A RELATIONSHIP is defined as: the way in which two or more concepts, objects, or people are connected, or the state of being connected. The state of being connected by blood or marriage.

Some synonyms for relationship: connection, relation, association, link, correlation, correspondence, parallel, alliance, bond, interrelation, interconnection

Some synonyms for family: family ties, family connections, blood ties, blood relationship, kinship, affinity, consanguinity, common ancestry, common lineage

Our greatest commandment from God is to LOVE. Love is one of the most profound emotions. The extending and receiving of love is often described as the most meaningful aspect of life, providing a source of deep fulfillment of great joy or immense pain. The establishment of a healthy, loving relationship is not innate but learned. Immense research has been done and the evidence suggests that the ability to form a stable relationship begins in infancy, in a child's earliest experiences. The ability of parents/caregivers to reliably meets the infant's needs for touch, food, care, safety, stimulation, and social interaction is fundamental to their development and appear to establish patterns for how we relate to others. Relationships require a willful commitment from all involved parties to do the required work in order for the relationship to grow healthily. The physical or emotional absence of a natural father, creates an internal void and strains one's ability to establish healthy relationship boundaries and communication, and therefore results in a struggle with intimacy.

How will you know if He heard you?
This requires relationship, engagement, connection, and on going communication. Call His name, He is available to you. He is our daddy, our Father, our GOD! He is the I AM, That I AM... There are so many ways to call or refer to our Daddy...

1. Almighty One – "...who is and who was and who is to come, the Almighty." Rev. 1:8

2. Alpha and Omega – "I am the Alpha and the Omega, the First and the Last, the Beginning and the End." Rev. 22:13

3. Advocate – "My dear children, I write this to you so that you will not sin. But if anybody does sin, we have an advocate with the Father—Jesus

Christ, the Righteous One." 1 John 2:1

4. <u>Author and Perfecter of Our Faith</u> – "Fixing our eyes on Jesus, the author and perfecter of faith, who for the joy set before Him endured the cross, despising the shame, and has sat down at the right hand of the throne of God." Heb. 12:2

5. <u>Authority</u> – "Jesus said, 'All authority in heaven and on earth has been given to me." Matt. 28:18

6. <u>Bread of Life</u> – "Then Jesus declared, 'I am the bread of life. Whoever comes to me will never go hungry, and whoever believes in me will never be thirsty.'" John 6:35

7. <u>Beloved Son of God</u> – "And behold, a voice from heaven said, "This is my beloved Son, with whom I am well pleased." Matt. 3:17

8. <u>Bridegroom</u> – "And Jesus said to them, "Can the wedding guests mourn as long as the bridegroom is with them? The days will come when the bridegroom is taken away from them, and then they will fast." Matt. 9:15

9. <u>Chief Cornerstone</u> – "The stone which the builders rejected has become the chief corner stone." Ps. 118:22

10. <u>Deliverer</u> – "And to wait for his Son from heaven, whom he raised from the dead, Jesus who delivers us from the wrath to come." 1 Thess.1:10

11. <u>Faithful and True</u> – "I saw heaven standing open and there before me was a white horse, whose rider is called Faithful and True. With justice he judges and wages war." Rev.19:11

12. <u>Good Shepherd</u> - "I am the good shepherd. The good shepherd lays down his life for the sheep." John 10:11

13. <u>Great High Priest</u> – "Therefore, since we have a great high priest who has passed through the heavens, Jesus the Son of God, let us hold fast our confession." Heb. 4:14

14. <u>Head of the Church</u> – "And he put all things under his feet and gave him as head over all things to the church." Eph. 1:22

15. <u>Holy Servant</u> – "…and grant that Your bond-servants may speak Your word with all confidence, while You extend Your hand to heal, and signs and wonders take place through the name of Your holy servant Jesus." Acts 4:29-30

16. <u>I Am</u> – "Jesus said to them, "Truly, truly, I say to you, before Abra-

ham was, I am." John 8:58

17. Immanuel – "...She will give birth to a son and will call him Immanuel, which means 'God with us.'" Is. 7:14

18. Indescribable Gift – "Thanks be to God for His indescribable gift." 2 Cor. 9:15

19. Judge – "...he is the one whom God appointed as judge of the living and the dead." Acts 10:42

20. King of Kings – "These will wage war against the Lamb, and the Lamb will overcome them, because He is Lord of lords and King of kings, and those who are with Him are the called and chosen and faithful." Rev. 17:14

21. Lamb of God – "The next day John saw Jesus coming toward him and said, "Look, the Lamb of God, who takes away the sin of the world!" John 1:29

22. Light of the World – "I am the light of the world. Whoever follows me will never walk in darkness, but will have the light of life." John 8:12

23. Lion of the Tribe of Judah – "Weep no more; behold, the Lion of the tribe of Judah, the Root of David, has conquered, so that he can open the scroll and its seven seals." Rev. 5:5

24. Lord of All – "For this reason also, God highly exalted Him, and bestowed on Him the name which is above every name, so that at the name of Jesus every knee will bow, of those who are in heaven and on earth and under the earth, and that every tongue will confess that Jesus Christ is Lord, to the glory of God the Father." Phil. 2:9-11

25. Mediator – "For there is one God, and one mediator between God and men, the man Christ Jesus." 1 Tim. 2:5

26. Messiah – "We have found the Messiah" (that is, the Christ)." John 1:41

27. Mighty One – "Then you will know that I, the Lord, am your Savior, your Redeemer, the Mighty One of Jacob." Is. 60:16

28. One Who Sets Free – "So if the Son sets you free, you will be free indeed." John 8:36

29. Our Hope – "...Christ Jesus our hope." 1 Tim. 1:1

30. Peace – "For he himself is our peace, who has made the two groups

one and has destroyed the barrier, the dividing wall of hostility," Eph. 2:14

31. Prophet – "And Jesus said to them, "A prophet is not without honor, except in his hometown and among his relatives and in his own household." Mark 6:4

32. Redeemer – "And as for me, I know that my Redeemer lives, and at the last He will take His stand on the earth." Job 19:25

33. Risen Lord – "...that Christ died for our sins according to the Scriptures, that he was buried, that he was raised on the third day according to the Scriptures." 1 Cor. 15:3-4

34. Rock – "For they drank from the spiritual Rock that followed them, and the Rock was Christ." 1 Cor. 10:4

35. Sacrifice for Our Sins – "This is love: not that we loved God, but that he loved us and sent his Son as an atoning sacrifice for our sins." 1 John 4:10

36. Savior – "For unto you is born this day in the city of David a Savior, who is Christ the Lord." Luke 2:11

37. Son of Man – "For the Son of Man came to seek and to save the lost." Luke 19:10

38. Son of the Most High – "He will be great and will be called the Son of the Most High. The Lord God will give him the throne of his father David." Luke 1:32

39. Supreme Creator Over All – "By Him all things were created, both in the heavens and on earth, visible and invisible, whether thrones or dominions or rulers or authorities-- all things have been created through Him and for Him. He is before all things, and in Him all things hold together...." 1 Cor. 1:16-17

40. Resurrection and the Life – "Jesus said to her, "I am the resurrection and the life. The one who believes in me will live, even though they die." John 11:25

41. The Door – "I am the door. If anyone enters by me, he will be saved and will go in and out and find pasture." John 10:9

42. The Way – "Jesus answered, "I am the way and the truth and the life. No one comes to the Father except through me." John 14:6

43. The Word – "In the beginning was the Word, and the Word was

with God, and the Word was God." John 1:1

44. <u>True Vine</u> – "I am the true vine, and My Father is the vinedresser." John 15:1

45. <u>Truth</u> – "And you will know the truth, and the truth will set you free." John 8:32

46. <u>Victorious One</u> – "To the one who is victorious, I will give the right to sit with me on my throne, just as I was victorious and sat down with my Father on his throne." Rev. 3:21

47. – 50. <u>Wonderful Counselor, Mighty God, Everlasting Father, Prince of Peace</u> – "For to us a child is born, to us a son is given, and the government will be on his shoulders. And he will be called Wonderful Counselor, Mighty God, Everlasting Father, Prince of Peace." Is. 9:6

All this... and so much more. He knows you! He knows you're His child. As my faith grows, I am confident in His ominpresence, and can rest knowing He is there.

Allowing Myself to be LIFTED UP

Chapter 7: Calling Out to Him

Commit to communicate-talk with Him, to Him and listen for His guidance and instructions. Will you allow yourself to be vulnerable and call out to Him openly and honestly, sharing your concerns, needs, and desires? Will you still yourself long enough to listen to Him and develop and intimate relationship with your Heavenly Father? Make a date with God and establish spending quality time with Him by choosing a day, time and place that you commit to showing up and being fully present. Do this 7 times and document the experience.

_____
_____
_____
_____
_____
_____
_____
_____
_____
_____
_____
_____
_____
_____
_____
_____
_____
_____
_____
_____

MY DECLARATION:

- ✓ I understand that relationship building takes time and I commit to dedicating time to build an intimate relationship with myself, God and the people I care about.

- ✓ I will allow myself to be open to exploring God's Word and learning how I can apply the 'Word' to my life.

CHAPTER 8

Resting on His Shoulders

Going Higher Expands Your Vision.

Make a decision to release your tie to negative past experiences that you have been holding on to. Cut the strings that are keeping you tied to your pain. Day by day; step by step commit to working on yourself. It is never too late to heal the wounds and cultivate a new story for your life. Recognize you are not alone. Healing the wounds and allowing yourself to be lifted, elevated, carried and release the need to control. Allow your daddy to lift you up.

During the past 27 years, of my professional career I have served in diverse roles as a counselor, case manager, program coordinator/manager, program director and grant developer for initiatives/programs serving "At-risk" youth and families living at or below poverty lines with proven barriers to self-sufficiency. I have had first-hand exposure to the traumatic experiences these groups endured and have seen the manifestation of trauma played out in their daily lives. I knew that I was passionate about the work I did because, "someone took time for me". That is what I would say. My work provided me with exposure to research and best practice approaches to serving the children and families. It was a workshop on Trauma Informed Care that began a journey of deeper self awareness and self-discovery for me. My understanding of the depth of childhood trauma that I was exposed to (that was never addressed) surfaced for me. I <u>am</u> the youth I serve; I understand and am personally familiar with the challenges that those parents and families face. I stepped into a realm of deeper awareness.

In trauma-informed practices, we learn to change the question about working with challenging youth from "What's wrong with you?" to "What happened to you?" It is a mind-shift, shifting the focus from blame to understanding. We don't have to know the details of the trauma in order to help. It's the asking of the question that helps us. Consider replacing "What happened to you?" with "I wonder what might you need?" My understanding grew. Behind every behavior is a need. This means we need to look at the experiences that shaped our beliefs. We have to commit to working on ourselves. To do our own work, unpack own our baggage and decide how we want to live and show up in the world. We have to decide that we want to live in an elevated place, where our vision, focus and outlook is not obstructed by our own perceptions of life.

What are we saying to ourselves, about ourselves? The things we tell ourselves shape our self-image and our beliefs and ultimately shape our actions.

Embracing this journey and surrendering to the process required me to unpack my baggage. I am experiencing what it feels like to be lifted up. I am free from the weight of the pain of my past. Cleansed from the feelings of shame. Layers of deeply embedded anger, pain, and disappointment have unraveled. I am resting on my Heavenly Father's shoulders; the sparkle of joy, wonder and excitement in my eyes, transformed, renewed I feel like I am soaring. I have clarity of vision. I hear His voice in my spirit and I now have the confidence to believe that I am truly worthy of hearing His voice. I am executing God's plan and purpose for my life. Join me in this experience of rebirth. I have entered a place of purpose focused rest in a space that I have not spent time before. People speak of the glow that radiates from me. I share that I am walking in obedience to God like never before. A peace and confidence in His love for me. As I reflected on my life while penning this book I stood in AWE of GOD! His presence, His faithfulness, His love, His Provision, His power and the manifestation of His Promise. I am here, standing and basking in His Glory I am a woman of value, worthy of loving and being loved.

Why does a child ask their daddy to lift them up? What is it that they are hoping for or expecting to see? What sparks their curiosity, desire, and interest to see beyond their own purview?

What a feeling of peace and rest knowing that you are safe. You can feel content, secure, confident, free from worry, because you know that He's got you.

Laughter, joy, peace, comfort and assurance, encompass me and keep me protected and free from harm. My safe place is where I am elevated from the vulnerable place where danger lurks. Many find meditation and worship is the place where they can go higher. I personally have found so much refuge in my personal place of worshipping God in song and prayer.

The song sung by Celine Dion entitled, "Because You Love Me", always touches me. The YOU in this song, to me, is my Heavenly Father. Because you love me Daddy, I am everything I am. The power and presence of Your love has brought healing to my soul.

Whether we fall or fail, when we cry or sob, we can rest assured that our daddy believes in us. He picks us up, brushes us off, and lets us try again. I'm everything I am, Because you love me! Daily I get to bask in the glory of Your love. Thank you DADDY!!!!

Allowing Myself to be LIFTED UP

Chapter 8: Resting on His Shoulders

In Position to SOAR: I am going higher and allowing myself to rest on His shoulders. I want to see and experience more. I am ready to release the weight of my past that has been holding me down. I asked to be LIFTED UP. I am allowing myself to be LIFTED UP. I trust that He can carry me. I embrace the experience to see beyond the obstacles before me because I have been elevated. My vision is expanded. I can see further than I could before. I commit to documenting this experience, rewriting my story and being an active participant in my healing process.

    Consider - Writing a letter to your earthly daddy; Write a letter to your heavenly daddy; write a letter to yourself. If a letter is too much for you,.. Purchase some post cards and send yourself words of encouragements in the mail. Put your list of affirming words and thoughts on a post-it and place it in a visible place to remind yourself that you are living from an elevated place.

MY DECLARATION:

- ✓ I stretch out my hand and reach out to be touched by GOD. I am grateful for His presence in my life. I know that He loves me. He lifts me. He carries me and I can rest safely in His arms or on His shoulders.

- ✓ I am covered. He supports me. He has never left me nor forsaken me.

- ✓ I am not alone... He has been there all the time!

Let Your Daddy Lift You Up

"Because You Loved Me" – Excerpt from Song by Celine Dion

For all those times you stood by me
For all the truth that you made me see
For all the joy you brought to my life
For all the wrong that you made right
For every dream you made come true
For all the love I found in you
I'll be forever thankful baby[JESUS]
You're the one who held me up
Never let me fall
You're the one who saw me through through it all

You were my strength when I was weak
You were my voice when I couldn't speak
You were my eyes when I couldn't see
You saw the best there was in me
Lifted me up when I couldn't reach
You gave me faith 'cause you believed

I'm everything I am
Because you loved me

Ooh, baby[JESUS]

You gave me wings and made me fly
You touched my hand, I could touch the sky
I lost my faith, you gave it back to me
You said no star was out of reach
You stood by me and I stood tall
I had your love, I had it all
I'm grateful for each day you gave me
Maybe I don't know that much
But I know this much is true
I was blessed because I was loved by you

Writer/s: DIANE WARREN
Publisher: Alfred, Walt Disney Music Company

He is waiting for you,
with open arms.

Will you let your heavenly
daddy lift you up?

About The Author

Arlene L. Connelly is a Life Enrichment Strategist and Servant Leader; who has dedicated over 25 years providing executive leadership, management, supervisory and administrative experiences in non-profit and higher education; serving adults, at-risk youth, families and underserved populations. She is a creative visionary who designs, develops, manages and evaluates programs.

She is a Certified John Maxwell Speaker/Trainer & Coach; Organizational and Leadership Development Professional; Healthy Relationships and Family Strengthening Coach; Career & Positive Youth Development Specialist, a Certified Global Career Development Facilitator and columnist for Shulamite Women Magazine.

Arlene is a community activist, she motivates individuals to action. She empowers parents, advocates for youth, and fund-raises for numerous causes. She is active in numerous community-building efforts. She serves on the Board of Directors for Daughters of Zion - Women of Destiny and Youth Speak Out International.

Ms. Connelly- is the Founder and CEO of ISEE GROUP, LLC an emerging Human Development Company whose mission is: "Restoring the Vision for Vibrant Relationships, Thriving Families & Stronger Communities." The company provides Consultation, Training, Coaching and Transformational Events & Experiences focused on Igniting in Individuals the Spirit to Excel in Excellence.

Arlene is driven, focused and steadfast in her walk with God. She has transformed pain into triumph and adversity into opportunity. Ms. Connelly has been a member of The Faith Center Ministries in Sunrise Florida, (a mega church with over 10,000 members), for more than 18 years and has served in various ministry roles providing leadership and strategic guidance.

A sought-after speaker who is not afraid to, "Tell It Like It Is", she is committed to motivating, coaching, and inspiring youth, adults and groups to assume their power, position and promise. By embracing and involving her audience at their life level, her focus is to impact the lives of others by word, example, and practice – with a most impressive track record to prove it. Ms. Connelly's enthusiastic demeanor coupled with her winning smile captivates those that are fortunate enough to be in her presence. Arlene is a mother to a beautiful daughter and a guiding light to countless people seeking mentoring, guidance and love.

WWW.ALCSPEAKS.COM

www.ingramcontent.com/pod-product-compliance
Lightning Source LLC
Chambersburg PA
CBHW052101110526
44591CB00013B/2299